How To Manage Your Time

For Katharine, James and Edmund

'Nothing really belongs to us but time,
which even he has who has nothing else.'

Baltasar Gracian.

'Time wasted is existence, used is life.'

Edward Young.

How To Manage Your Time

John Adair

Talbot Adair

Published by
The Talbot Adair Press
Newlands, Pewley Hill
Guildford, Surrey GU1 3SN, England

Second impression 1987
Third impression 1988

British Library Cataloguing in Publication Data

Adair, John, *1934–*
    How To Manage Your Time
    1. Executives—Time management
    I. Title
    658.4'093   HD38.2

ISBN 0 9511835 0 8

Typeset by Optichrome Ltd, Woking, Surrey
Printed and bound in Great Britain by
Biddles Ltd, Guildford and King's Lynn

Contents

page

INTRODUCTION

1. TIME MANAGEMENT IN PERSPECTIVE   3

   The Nature of Time
   A Clockwork Revolution
   Time is like Money
   Key Points

2. COMMON TIME PROBLEMS   13

   The Case of the Procrastinator
   The Case of the Poor Delegator
   The Case of the Office Mismanager
   The Case of the Ineffective Chairman
   The Case of the Undirected Trainer
   Time Management — A Personal Challenge
   Key Points

3. DEVELOPING A PERSONAL SENSE OF TIME   27

   Keeping a Time Log
   Review and Reflect
   What Happens to a Manager's Time?
   Key Points

4. HOW TO IDENTIFY LONG-TERM GOALS   35

Life Planning in Perspective
To Live is to Journey Forwards
Know Your Values
The Nature of Policy
Key Points

5. HOW TO MAKE MIDDLE-TERM PLANS   45

Time Budgeting
What an Operational Plan should do for you
Characteristics of Goals and Objectives
Time Norms for Routine Activities
The Quarterly Review
Key Points

6. PLANNING THE DAY   55

Attitudes to Time
Begin with the Year's Diary
The Daily List
Learn to Say No
The Time Fanatic
Key Points

7. MAKING BEST USE OF YOUR BEST TIME   67

What is your Best Time?
How to be More Creative
Moonlighting
The Pareto Principle
Key Points

8. TIME EFFECTIVENESS IN OFFICES   77

    Office Arrangement
    The Art of Deskmanship
    Paperwork
    How to Write and Read Effectively
    Make the Telephone Work for You
    How to Control Interruptions
    Your Professional Assistant
    Key Points

9. MANAGING MEETINGS   93

    Different Kinds of Meetings
    The Cost of Meeting
    Preparing for an Effective Meeting
    Timetabling the Meeting
    The Chairman's Role
    The Art of Minuting
    A Self-Development Exercise
    Key Points

10. THE ART OF DELEGATION   111

    Difficulties of Delegation
    What Cannot be Delegated
    Developing Your Skills as a Delegator
    Key Points

11. MAKING USE OF COMMITTED TIME   127

    Daily Routines
    Waiting Time
    Travel Time
    Television
    Key Points

12. ON HEALTH AND HOLIDAYS   135

Your Energy Bank Balance
Get Enough Sleep
Commonsense Diet
Take Exercise
The Importance of Holidays
Practical Meditation
Coping with Stress
Key Points

SUMMARY: TEN STEPS TOWARDS BETTER TIME MANAGEMENT
151

APPENDICES   153

BIBLIOGRAPHY   157

INDEX   159

Introduction

Time is a scarce resource. It is irreplaceable and irreversible. Few things are more important to us than learning how to save time and how to spend it wisely.

This principle applies to us all in most areas of our lives. But it is especially true in the world of work. For there the potential demands and pressures on our time greatly outweigh what is available. We have to choose our ends wisely and manage our time and abilities carefully to achieve them.

This book is about time management, in relation to life generally and to work in particular. Business executives, doctors, engineers, teachers are among many now aware of the need to manage time better. But there is an understandable scepticism about facile systems which promise complete control over time. There should always be sensitive response to the time needs of others. Over-preoccupation with one's own time is not an attractive quality. Moreover, the management of time can never be seen in isolation. It is only one of the elements of effective performance.

Paradoxically, to save time you must spend time. Budget some of your time now — perhaps on a forthcoming journey or quietly at home — to read this book as a step towards better time management. Regard it as an investment which will pay rich dividends by helping you to:

Develop a new personal sense of time

Think about the future, set goals and develop plans

Analyse where, how and why you are spending your time at present

Reduce time pressures

Rid yourself of activities which waste time

Learn how to save time by delegating

Re-allocate your time to produce better results

Learn time-saving techniques in meetings, reading, correspondence, travel, telephone calls and scheduling appointments

Use more time to think creatively

Find time to relax and enjoy life

Make time an ally instead of an enemy

1. Time Management In Perspective

"What is time? How did the concept of time management arise? What is the relation of time management to life as a whole?"

These are not easy questions to answer. Possibly for that reason they are ignored by most other books on time management. Let us not make that mistake. For the attempt to view time management in its historical perspective may yield some important insights.

This chapter invites you to identify your assumptions about time management. How far are they *your* beliefs, consciously adopted and held? You may find that some of them are more or less unconscious assumptions, picked up from our common history and culture. For we inherit a tradition. It helps if we understand that tradition and build upon the foundations.

THE NATURE OF TIME

A sense of time as transitory is deeply human. As far as we know, animals do not experience it. *Tempus fugit* — Time flies — is a universal refrain. But what is time? Ancient philosophers were as much puzzled as we are:

'For what is Time? Who is able easily and briefly to explain it? Who is able so much as to comprehend it in thought as to

express himself concerning it? And yet what in our usual dis-
course do we more familiarly and knowingly make more
mention of than Time? And surely we understand it well
enough when we speak of it; we understand it also when in
speaking with another we hear it named. What then is Time? If
nobody asks me I know; but if I wanted to explain it to someone that should ask me, plainly I do not know'.

Things have not changed much since St. Augustine wrote
those words. We all know what we mean by time but we cannot
say what it is. Philosophers and physicists are less sure, for their
speculations and calculations do not throw more light on the
matter.

If you are travelling at a speed faster than another person,
time will go slower for you. If you flew around the world at 500
miles per hour with an atomic clock on the seat beside you,
when you returned to where you started your clock would be
about one hundredth of a millionth of a second slower than its
twin on the ground.

Einstein's discovery of this relativity provoked much
thought about the relations of the dimensions of time and
space. At very great speeds time does go slower. For general or
everyday purposes, however, Einstein's discovery adds nothing
to our understanding of time, for we don't travel at the kind of
speed he had in mind. But Einstein has added to the mystery
of time.

The nearest we can come to grasping the concept of time is
to look upon it as a dimension, like space. It is the dimension in
which change happens. The *rate* of change varies enormously:
mountains form and crumble over millions of years while men
are born and die over decades. Being human we tend to
measure time and change in terms of our life span.

Although we know that each hour actually has sixty minutes
and each minute sixty seconds, we experience time in different
ways. Sometimes we are not aware of it at all. Sometimes it
goes faster and sometimes slower. Time has its own psychology.

'No young man believes he shall ever die', wrote William
Hazlitt. There is a feeling of eternity in youth; perhaps the
young are prodigal with time because they feel they have so

much of it. Yet boredom, not knowing what to do with time, can be the other side of the coin.

As we advance in life, we acquire a keener sense of the value of time. For some people nothing else, indeed, seems of any consequence; and in this respect they become misers. But for others time can again hang heavy. For a very old person sitting in hospital waiting to go home, time can seem like eternity. Yet for such a person, paradoxically, there may be only days or hours of time left.

Time often seems to me to go more slowly in the dark than in the light, just as time waiting for dentists or trains drags its feet.

There are other illusions. Generally, when we are looking forward intensely to something, the shorter the time the longer it seems to us. Is that because we measure it in shorter units? Or simply because we are conscious of time and think about measuring it?

Time spent in purposeful activity can fly past. That may be why, as we grow older, time seems to be speeding up — years go by faster, days are like hours, and hours minutes. That is, providing we are busy.

Time management is most likely to be attractive to busy people.

A CLOCKWORK REVOLUTION

The ordinary man is not bothered by our comparative ignorance about the nature of time. What matters to him is that he can measure time. If, like the great majority of the world's population, in this century as in previous ones, he lives by farming or herding, his time is measured for him by natural events: dawn, sunrise, high noon, sunset and nightfall. He needs no more accurate measure for his daily activities. We all live by nature's clock. Day follows night; season follows season. These cycles are stamped upon us.

Why, then, do we need clocks? Who needs them? Even the most ancient and most natural of artificial clocks — the sundial — can seem an intruder on the business of living. David Landes in his history of time measurement aptly entitled *Revo-*

lution in Time (1983) quotes an actor's amusing lament from a
play performed in ancient Rome:

> 'The gods confound the man who first found out
> How to distinguish hours. Confound him, too,
> Who in this place set up a sundial,
> To cut and hack my days so wretchedly
> Into small pieces! When I was a boy,
> My belly was my sundial — one surer,
> Truer, and more exact than any of them.
> This dial told me when 'twas the proper time
> To go to dinner, when I ought to eat,
> But nowadays, why even when I have,
> I can't fall to unless the sun gives leave.
> The town's so full of these confounded dials . . .'

The sundial as a form of clock had grave limitations. It
would not work in countries where clouds obscured the sun for
much of the year. By the end of the fourteenth century some
ingenious Europeans succeeded in inventing mechanical
clocks, complete with a series of gear wheels driven by weights.
Fitted only with an hour hand and lacking in accuracy, they yet
served both to show the time and strike it out on bells in
churches and city squares. The clock next to St. Mark's
Cathedral in Venice is a fine surviving example.

Gradually clocks became smaller, until relatively wealthy
people could own a portable clock for domestic use. The key
technological step was the invention of the coiled spring, which
could be made even smaller. From table clocks the European
craftsmen developed the pocket watch. Not until the 1860s did
the Swiss mass-produce a reliable cheap watch for the man in
the street. Not until the First World War did wristwatches become popular.

Meanwhile, clocks became ever more accurate, measuring
minutes and seconds. Harrison's Chronometer (1671) lost or
gained no more than one second a day. Only the recent introduction of the quartz technology has brought that degree of
accuracy to the common household clock and wristwatch. It
means that you can now measure your time in seconds.
Today's atomic clocks are much more accurate than that.

TIME DISCIPLINE

A commercial sense of time — time is money — seems to have been born among the Italian merchants of the late Middle Ages. It was mixed with the religious concern inculcated by the Church and heightened by the haunting imminence of death. Few reached their allotted span of three score years and ten.

The Black Death wiped out between a quarter and a third of the population in the century of the first mechanical clocks. Life was short and uncertain: death stood at one's shoulder. Therefore time must be used to the full.

Leon Alberti was a partner in a firm of Italian merchants in the early fifteenth century whose correspondence has survived. From his letters it is clear that young Alberti deserves to be recognized as a pioneer of modern time management. 'In the morning when I get up', he wrote, 'the first thing I do is think to myself: what am I going to do today? So many things: I count them, think about them, and to each I assign its time.' He continued, 'I'd rather lose sleep than time, in the sense of the proper time for doing what has to be done.' Sleep, eating and the like could always be done tomorrow, but not today's business. Alberti set himself 'to watch the time, and assign things by time, to devote oneself to business and never lose an hour of time.' With the excitement of a man who has glimpsed a great truth he concludes: 'He who knows how not to waste time can do just about anything; and he who knows how to make use of time will be lord of whatever he wants.'

The English Puritan preachers in particular gave practical instructions in plain language to their congregations on how to save time and use it. For example, they advocated the keeping of journals or diaries as a means of daily self-examination, thereby creating a practical time management tool. They advocated the daily planning of time. Lay Puritans heeded the message. For example, Sir Matthew Hale, a Puritan judge in Restoration England, used to begin each day by sitting down after prayers and making a careful plan for the day ahead.

It is no surprise, then, that Protestants led the way in the manufacture of pocket watches, especially in France and Switzerland. Where people had once relied upon the night watchman's cry, the tolling of church bells, or the striking turret clock in the market square, now they could *watch* the time at home or on their person. Lives could not be ordered in a style once reserved for monastic communities. Time became more personal.

All those activities which depend on people meeting and parting could now be organised by the clock. Generals could synchronize the great movements of troops; railways could be run in accordance with complicated timetables. None of this was possible before the widespread use of clocks and watches.

'Remember that time is money,' wrote Benjamin Franklin in *Advice to a Young Tradesman* (1745). In 1723 Franklin had run away from his Puritan parents in New England, but not before he had imbibed the Puritan virtues of thrift, industry and conscientiousness. The sons and grandsons of the Puritans, breathing the more secular air of the eighteenth century, did not abandon the principle of managing time. They changed the ends. In place of the glory and enjoyment of God in this world and the next, they substituted the mundane pursuits of wealth, health and happiness. 'Do you love life?' asks Franklin. 'Then do not squander time, for that is the stuff life is made of.'

TIME IS LIKE MONEY

Time discipline, then, can be applied to any ends. It is a transferable skill. In history there has been a shift from religious to secular ends — especially the making of money. That is not irreversible. There is no reason why the principles of time management now taught in a business context cannot be applied to spiritual and intellectual life. For example, the businessman's proverb — time is money — can help us towards a personal philosophy of time.

Human understanding advances partly by the use of analogy. This is especially true when it comes to talking about such abstractions as time. Franklin was not the first to compare time to money, but since his day it has become the most common analogy. It is worth reflecting carefully about it.

Both time and money are limited resources. That's the point of the analogy. Therefore time (like money) is a valuable commodity. It can be borrowed, saved or squandered — all words springing from the original and basic analogy. Indeed there is a whole system of smaller metaphors under the 'Time is money' umbrella, such as:

> Yesterday is a cancelled cheque
> Tomorrow is a promissory note
> Today is ready cash. Use it!

The invention of banks, virtually unknown in Puritan days, adds another dimension to the analogy. Our forefathers pictured time as a bald old man with a forelock, carrying a scythe and an hourglass. Perhaps today we would imagine Father Time as a bank manager, threatening us with a notice of our impending total bankruptcy and turning towards us a quartz clock on his table.

All analogies break down at a certain point. Time is patently *not* money. It is only when we begin to think about the ways in which it is not money that our sense of its uniqueness comes home. You can make money; you can't make time. Money isn't finite. Sand in the hourglass is not like money in the bank. As the Chinese proverb says, 'An inch of gold cannot buy an inch of time.' Time is really infinitely *more* precious than money.

The 'Time is money' analogy is operational, not a mere literary ornament. It is a positive and practical help to look upon time as money. For money is a widespread yardstick of value. If we see our time as being *more* valuable than money we have it about right. As most of us try to save our money and invest it wisely how much more should we try to avoid wasting our time and to invest it with energy to good effect?

Arnold Bennett's book *How to Live on Twenty-Four Hours a Day*, published in 1907, ran through fourteen editions in the United States. Although Bennett was mainly concerned to prove that a clerk commuting daily to the City of London could find plenty of time to read good books if he chose to manage his time well, the same principle could be applied once again to money-making. Henry Ford gave 500 copies of Bennett's book to his managers; another American motor company president issued 18,000 copies, one to each employee.

THE DAILY MIRACLE

Philosophers have explained space. They have not explained time. It is the inexplicable raw material of everything. With it, all is possible; without it, nothing. The supply of time is truly a daily miracle, an affair genuinely astonishing when one examines it. You wake up in the morning, and lo! your purse is magically filled with twenty-four hours of the unmanufactured tissue of the universe of your life! It is yours. It is the most precious of possessions. A highly singular commodity, showered upon you in a manner as singular as the commodity itself!

For remark! No one can take it from you. It is unstealable. And no one receives either more or less than you receive.

Talk about an ideal democracy! In the realm of time there is no aristocracy of wealth, and no aristocracy of intellect. Genius is never rewarded by even an extra hour a day. And there is no punishment. Waste your infinitely precious commodity as much as you will, and the supply will never be withheld from you. No mysterious power will say:– "This man is a fool, if not a knave. He does not deserve time; he shall be cut off at the meter." It is more certain than government bonds, and payment of income is not affected by Sundays. Moreover, you cannot draw on the future. Impossible to get into debt! You can only waste the passing moment. You cannot waste tomorrow; it is kept for you. You cannot waste the next hour; it is kept for you.

I said the affair was a miracle. Is it not?

You have to live on this twenty-four hours of daily time. Out of it you have to spin health, pleasure, money, content, respect, and the evolution of your immortal soul. Its right use, its most effective use, is a matter of the highest urgency and of the most thrilling actuality. All depends on that.

Arnold Bennett

The 'Time is money' analogy is central to Bennett's argument. 'Why not concern yourself more with "How to live on a given income of time", instead of "How to live on a given income of money!" Money is far commoner than time,' he writes. 'When one reflects, one perceives that money is just about the commonest thing there is. The supply of time, though gloriously regular, is cruelly restricted.

Which of us lives on twenty-four hours a day? And when I say "lives" I do not mean exists, nor "muddles through". Which of us is free from that uneasy feeling that the "great spending departments" of his daily life are not managed as they ought to be? Which of us is not saying to himself — which of us has not been saying to himself all his life: "I shall alter that when I have a little more time."

We never shall have any more time. We have, and we have always had, all the time there is.'

The realization of this 'profound and neglected truth', as Bennett called it, should lead us to examine, in subsequent chapters, how time is wasted and to formulate some practical steps for improving our use of it.

KEY POINTS

● Time is as mysterious as space. It is the dimension in which changes happen, balanced by relative continuities.

● Time can be measured with exceptional accuracy by clocks. Mechanical clocks have a profound influence on us. They make us even more time-conscious than our ancestors, although our increased life expectancy may make us less so in other respects.

● Clocks exert a discipline upon us. The Puritans in particular inculcated in Britain and America a sense of the preciousness of time and the sinfulness of wasting it. Thrift, industry and punctuality go hand-in-hand.

● Not everyone operates on the 'Time is money' analogy. Actually time is infinitely more valuable than money. It deserves to be treated with even greater respect.

● Only when you have perceived and assigned the right value to your time — more than gold or silver — are you able to benefit from the practical suggestions in the remaining chapters of this book. A fresh realization of the intrinsic worth of your time engenders a burning desire in you to use it well.

It is not possible to hold the day.
It is possible not to lose it.
Sundial, 1695

2. Common Time Problems

Look in a mirror and you will see your biggest time waster. Until you come to grips with that reality, few if any of your personal time problems will be overcome.

Ironically, the worst offenders are often those who seem to be working hardest and longest. They may appear very busy but they are not very effective. They do not manage their time well.

, This chapter aims to help you to identify some of your own and other people's major time problems and their causes. You may see yourself in the five case studies. They are like mirrors which are being held up for that purpose. If you do recognize yourself in one or two — or even all — of them, do not despair. Awareness and self-understanding are the first steps towards a complete cure. The whole of this book is intended to enable you to acquire good time management habits.

THE CASE OF THE PROCRASTINATOR

Robert Deal was potentially a good manager in many ways, especially in his relations with his staff. But they found his habit of procrastination infuriating. Even with minor matters he tended to postpone decisions until tomorrow — and tomorrow never comes. His two subordinates sometimes came out of his office complaining to each other, "He has all the information we can afford to get and now is the time for decision but, once more, it's back to us for more work." Mr. Deal was not incapable of decisiveness, however; he had just slipped into the habit of putting things off until tomorrow. This was especially noticeable when he was faced with unpleasant matters. Standards had been slipping in the office. A major personnel problem needed to be sorted out. Both issues were shelved until a more convenient time, but the time never seemed right. Reports, letters, and urgent requests piled up on his table. In the end this habit of procrastination proved his undoing. Typically he delayed reading a letter of warning about a forthcoming meeting, and went unprepared into the lion's den. The new chief executive fired him after the meeting.

Procrastination is often the vice of people who like to consider work rather than actually do it. As one of the characters in Jerome K. Jerome's *Three Men in a Boat* said, "I like work; it fascinates me. I can sit and look at it for hours. I love to keep it by me: the idea of getting rid of it nearly breaks my heart."

What is procrastination? How does it differ from, say, delaying a decision until more information is available? It can best be defined as putting off the doing of something that should be done — *intentionally, habitually and reprehensibly*.

If you suspect that you are prone to procrastination always ask yourself "*Why* am I putting this off?" If you can see no good reason — and don't confuse reasons with excuses — brace yourself and take action this day. 'Never leave that till tomorrow which you can do today,' wrote Benjamin Franklin.

Procrastination will mean you are just about keeping up with last week's business. By off-loading today's work onto tomorrow you are simply storing up work for yourself. Tomorrow becomes the busiest day of the week.

Avoid delays! Resolve not to postpone what is ready to be done today. There is no time like the present. Wellington ascribed his unbroken victories as a general to 'doing the day's business in the day'.

Be suspicious of yourself or others when deferment or delay is counselled. It may be just one more step on the road to dilatoriness. A wise person will indeed delay certain decisions or actions: there may genuinely be insufficient information or commitment. But he will never be in love with tomorrow, that most uncertain of all time's corridors.

You won't have heard of James Albery (1838-1889). As far

as I know he achieved absolutely nothing. I am not sure if he even got around to writing his own epitaph. If not, someone who knew him well, penned a perfect summary of a born procrastinator:

> He slept beneath the moon,
> He basked beneath the sun.
> He lived a life of going-to-do
> And died with nothing done.

Procrastination, which comes from the Latin word for 'tomorrow' is the world's number one time-waster. As the proverb says, it is 'the thief of time'. You must banish it from your life if you want to become a better time manager. Be tough with yourself. Start now by doing something today that you have been putting off. It may be a small or large matter: an overdue apology; a confrontation with a low performer; a meeting with your boss; or an unpleasant task you know you should tackle. The most difficult job of the day may not turn out as fearsome as you imagined.

THE CASE OF THE POOR DELEGATOR

The Chairman, back from New Zealand that afternoon, suddenly summoned Tom Saunders, his Chief Executive, from his weekly management meeting. He pulled out the latest American paperback book called *How to Delegate* from his briefcase and gave it to Tom. "That's your problem, Tom. You are carrying too much of the load of this company on your own shoulders. Read it by the end of next week and we'll have dinner at my club and talk about it."

Tom returned to the meeting fuming. "As if I haven't got enough work," he erupted. "Now the Chairman has given me a book to read. Where were we? Yes, I was asking you about the grade of oil I told you to use in the . . ."

"Hold on, Tom," said Stephen Barnes, the Finance Director. "I think the Chairman has got a point. No one works harder than you, Tom, but you do get over-attentive to details on the technical side. James is quite capable of handling them — it's his job — especially on the salary we are paying him! You do tend to interfere with those you have delegated responsibilities to, or at least it seems so to us. It's as if you don't quite trust us. And you waste a lot of your own valuable time checking administrative details and even doing a mass of routine work that others could do for you. If you did delegate more that would give you time to think about where this company is going in the next few years. And you might avoid a second coronary."

"You seem to have got everyone nodding in agreement with you, you old bastard Stephen," said Tom Saunders with a smile. "All right, I'll read the bloody book — if I have time over the weekend with all this to do." He tapped his bulging briefcase expressively. "Now, about that oil . . ."

Delegation saves your time and develops subordinates. It does not save the organisation's time, for someone else's time is being used. But it improves results by making fuller use of resources.

Failure to delegate eats your time. Again, always ask "Why am I not delegating?" Try to dig down to the real reason. Sometimes a manager is more comfortable doing the work of his subordinates: it is less challenging or threatening than the tasks he should be tackling himself.

Delegation implies transferring initiative and authority to another for performance of agreed tasks. The subordinate should have the necessary competence for the job, together with a willingness to accept it. You should retain a means of exercising overall control and checking performance. Both of you — superior and subordinate — share a sense of responsibility for what has now become a common task.

If the task to be delegated is relatively novel you should consider beforehand what new knowledge and skills will be needed. Developing your key individuals by training and counselling is part of your core responsibility as a leader. Delegation crowns the process of developing staff: it is the seal of recognition, respect and trust.

Delegation implies good subordinates. Poor ones prefer to have their thinking done for them. They will always be pestering you for decisions or answers they could provide themselves. Never let them come to you with problems unless they bring their proposed solutions as well. Nine times out of ten you will be able to say, "Fine, go and do it." Eventually they will get the message and only come to you on the tenth occasion, when help from you is genuinely needed. For it will be something that only you can do.

Watch out for the phenomenon of upward delegation. Tom Saunders, the manager in the above case study whom I knew well, was especially prone to accept jobs from his subordinates. These were tasks they ought to have done themselves. Usually they 'bounced' these chores onto Tom when they met him in the corridor or the lift. Being a willing work horse and wanting to be helpful he rarely said no. But he certainly learnt his lesson after reading that book on delegation. I tried to get him to write up that case study but he told me to do it myself!

Delegate as much as you can. Recognise also now that there is an art in delegation. It is simple but it is not easy. Chapter 9 explores the whole subject more fully. If you want to acquire the most important *strategic* time-saver, you must master the art of delegation.

CHECKLIST — DO YOU NEED TO DELEGATE MORE?	YES	NO
Are you frequently interrupted by subordinates with questions about the job or requests for advice and/or decisions?	☐	☐
Do you sometimes find yourself doing the job of one of your subordinates when he really ought to be doing it himself?	☐	☐
Do you work longer hours than those you manage?	☐	☐
Do you habitually take work home every night or at weekends?	☐	☐
Are you always rushed off your feet?	☐	☐
Do you set standards so high that only you can attain them?	☐	☐

Are you a constant 'checker-upper', keeping a
close watch on the details of how the delegate is
doing the job?   □   □

Do you have unfinished jobs piling up on your
desk, or difficulty in meeting deadlines?   □   □

Does more of your time get spent in working on
details rather than on strategic thinking, planning
and other key leadership functions?   □   □

If so, do you work at details because you enjoy
them, although someone else could look after
them well enough?   □   □

Has anyone in the last year described you as
being 'too conscientious' or 'rather too much of a
perfectionist'?   □   □

Do you lack confidence in your staff's abilities
and experience so that you are frankly afraid to
risk giving them more decision-making powers?   □   □

THE CASE OF THE OFFICE MISMANAGER

Henry Wilson shuffled through the papers piled high on his
desk. "This office looks like a rummage sale," he sighed, briefly
surveying the files, books, letters and unfinished contracts lit-
tering the floor and covering every available surface. "Ah, here
it is . . . now, where's my pen." He sat down to write a reply, but
was interrupted by Bill Jenkins for ten minutes about some
minor matter over the Nigerian contract. His secretary then
brought in a pile of unopened mail for him to sort through, but
the telephone began to ring and Henry answered all nine calls
himself. One wrong number, two wrong departments and
another minor query from Bill, who still hadn't got his act
together on the Nigerian order. Then it was coffee time, which
took up another thirty or forty minutes, not least because
Nancy his secretary wanted to tell him all about what the vet
had said about her Dobermann Pinscher.

There was just time before lunch to deal with five telephone
calls and to carry out another search among his papers for a

missing telephone number. The afternoon was worse, with people dropping in without appointments or telephoning at will for a chat. By 5.30 p.m. Henry had just about completed a short memo on stockpiling raw materials which had been due to be sent last week. Just before he left for home he found five of the morning's letters, still unopened. One of them turned out to be a cancellation of the Nigerian project that everyone had assumed was going to happen — and Bill wasted an hour of his time about. Apparently the Nigerians had found a West German firm that could promise to deliver the equipment on schedule. They were weary of the delays they had experienced with Wilson's firm. "The trouble is, Nancy," said Henry Wilson as he stuffed the letters into his briefcase, "there aren't enough hours in the day. God gave me only twenty-four hours a day — everyone else seems to have more."

Henry Wilson is totally disorganised. He is snowed under with paperwork. He thinks he is busy but he isn't really. Interruptions in person or by telephone fragment his day, leaving him little time to achieve anything. When he goes home he often asks himself: "What have I *done* today? What have I *achieved*?" The answer is usually nothing very much. Henry blames it all on not having enough hours in the day. But if he organised himself and his office better he would find he had all the time he needs.

To deal effectively with paperwork you need a system. Chapter 7 sets out some advice on that score. Since the invention of the photocopier you are engaged in a battle for survival against the tide of papers that floods your office or rushes through the letter box. Only a ruthless policy of spending the minimum time possible on a piece of paper — handling it only once if possible — will save you from total ineffectiveness.

Your secretary, if you have one, should be competent enough to organise and run the administrative side of your office life. She should open the mail and sort it out according to some system of priority. She should screen your incoming calls and visitors to deflect the obvious time-wasters.

Answer the following questions honestly. If in doubt, ask your secretary to check your answers — it may lead to a constructive dialogue.

CHECKLIST —
MANAGING TIME IN THE OFFICE   YES NO

Are routine tasks in the office crowding out time
I should be spending on urgent and important
priorities?   ☐   ☐

Do I find myself constantly worrying about
trivia?   ☐   ☐

Could I cut out some of the interruptions to my
work each day?   ☐   ☐

Do I *like* interruptions, however irrelevant to my
main concerns?   ☐   ☐

Are my desk and office in good order, with 'a
place for everything and everything in its place'?   ☐   ☐

Does my secretary act as a professional assistant,
as opposed to being merely a typist?   ☐   ☐

Muddle makes work and wastes time. Strive for good order in your office. Establish systems for dealing with the predictable and maintain them. Then you will find that you are free for the unpredictables — be they problems, crises or opportunities.

THE CASE OF THE INEFFECTIVE CHAIRMAN

As an outstanding biologist Sally Hodson won promotion as Head of the Department of Microbiology at Jenner University at the young age of 32. Without any training in leadership she found herself trying to run a large department of 16 academic staff, 8 technical assistants, an administrative officer, secretaries and typists, as well as keeping up her own teaching and pursuing her important research. Meetings of all kinds — research group, departmental, faculty, university — seemed to fill the term, while meetings of another sort — conferences — occupied some of the vacations. At home there were yet more meetings: parents' associations, school governors, parish councils. More often than not Sally found herself made chairman, usually because no one else wanted the job. Sally was in such a perpetual hurry that she didn't find time to prepare for meetings. Papers seldom arrived with the agenda — if there was one. "Most meetings are a waste of time," she told her husband. "Half the time is spent discussing what is the object of the meeting. Usually it's a question of too many people — often the wrong ones at that — talking too much about too little."

"Why don't you do something about it then?" grunted her husband from the depths of the newspaper. He was familiar with her litany of complaints about meetings.

"What *can* I do?" said Sally. "People arrive late or leave early. As for the agenda they jump around all over the place, never sticking to the subject. Trivial items, like the departmental notepaper, can take an hour. Next year's research budget is dismissed in five minutes. It's hopeless. Meetings drag on for two hours or more. And then no one ever seems to know what was agreed, let alone do anything about it."

What do you think Sally Hodson could do about her meetings? She is caught in a time trap herself. But she is also wasting other people's time. She postpones meetings without consideration. Agendas are chopped and changed. There is inadequate preparation beforehand. Lack of control allows discussion to meander unchecked. Lastly, you notice that there are inadequate minutes, so that action after her meetings was usually confused.

Meetings of all kinds — formal committees to informal meetings of two or three people in your room — involve others. Therefore they are a potential time threat. For others can take up your time in wasteful ways if you are not careful, especially if they are nominally in control of the meeting. Always agree a time budget for a meeting of any sort and keep to it if possible.

Get into the habit of asking questions about meetings. Preferably you should do so *before* they happen. Here are seven key questions:

● What would happen if we didn't have this meeting?

● Why are we meeting?

● What is the end product of this meeting?

● How long do we need for it?

● Who should be there?

● How can it be best structured?

● When should it be held — is this the right time for it?

Unless you can satisfactorily answer these questions *do not hold the meeting.* Meetings are designed to save time. As chairman or member, you have a vital part to play to see that meetings begin and end on time, and accomplish their tasks in the most time-effective way.

THE CASE OF THE UNDIRECTED TRAINER

Liz Fellows works in staff training in Midminster, one of the large clearing banks. A year ago she joined a group of about 30 trainers in a new group set up to provide a more comprehensive training service for managers and supervisors. She became increasingly frustrated by planning courses that were either cancelled or failed to attract enough participants. She complained to her manager: "We are wasting a lot of time because we don't know what our aims and objectives are. What are we trying to do? I feel as if I am working in the dark."

"So do I," said her manager. "At head office they keep changing our priorities. This month it's our customer service campaign. The month before it they were on about training for information technology. We have achieved some of our objectives, but no one can tell me what we are supposed to be doing at present. No one gives me a strategy or some policy guidelines, Liz, and so I can't help you."

Liz Fellows went away in a thoughtful mood. That evening she told her husband, "I am not even sure now I am in the right job."

With her enthusiasm dimmed and her morale low she began to look elsewhere for another job. She now works as a saleswoman in a department store. "At least I know the objective now," she told her former manager when she met him in the street. "Lucky you," he replied, "it's still the same confusion at the Midminster."

It is difficult to manage your time effectively if you are not as clear as possible about your purpose, aims and objectives. Many organisations and work groups do not have a grasp of their 'core mission', let alone the more definite aims and objectives which should be channelling their sense of purpose in daily activity.

Within that framework you need a sense of priority — what needs to be done next. There are elaborate schemes in some textbooks on time management for what has come to be called 'prioritising' — an ugly addition to the English language but nevertheless a useful one. To arrive at your priority rating for anything, however, you have to ask yourself two simple questions:

● How *important* is it?

● How *urgent* is it?

A priority may have different mixes of those two ingredients, which you can distinguish without too much difficulty:

Exercise

Review your priorities at present and list them (not more than five) in a single column. Now grade them in order according to *importance* A, B, C, D or E. On the other side grade them according to *urgency* 1, 2, 3, 4 or 5.

Now re-list them according to their composite scores. There is no system for doing it, such as rating B4 higher than C1. You have to use your judgement.

Whether in personal or professional life it pays to be clear about your aims and goals. That again sounds simple, but in practice it is difficult to obtain the necessary degree of clarity. Yet the fruit of clarity is that time management will become natural for you. You will have ceased to suffer from perhaps the most chronic time management problem of all — unclear objectives.

TIME MANAGEMENT — A PERSONAL CHALLENGE

Reading the above five case studies may have prompted you to identify some of your own symptoms as a poor time manager. Once you have identified those areas for improvement you can begin to build a programme for change.

Improving your effectiveness in the use of time is like trying to become a better golf player. The perfect score is 18, a hole in one 18 consecutive times. Obviously it is most improbable that anyone will ever achieve that score, but that doesn't stop keen golfers from endlessly trying to improve their game. In the process they may learn humility. As you strive to work economically and achieve more in your time, set yourself a similar aim. Perfection may elude you, but excellence is within your grasp.

Why not turn over a new leaf? It is never too late to make a fresh beginning. You should be in no doubt, however, that it is an exceptionally difficult task to become a good manager of your own and other people's time. Don't let the difficulty of it put you off, but regard it rather as a challenge.

Goethe once remarked that writers begin books but readers finish them. If I could rephrase that, this book can offer the signposts and road maps of better time management, but you must supply the motive power.

Pause for a moment and ask yourself: "Do I really *want* to manage my time better? Am I prepared to pay the price of investing some time in reading and re-reading these chapters, answering the checklists and making notes for action? Will I undertake to review my practical self-improvement programme every month for six months?

ON TURNING OVER A NEW LEAF

The most important preliminary to the task of arranging one's life so that one may live fully and comfortably within one's daily budget of twenty-four hours is the calm realization of the extreme difficulty of the task, of the sacrifices and the endless effort which it demands. I cannot too strongly insist on this.

If you imagine that you will be able to achieve your ideal by ingeniously planning out a time-table with a pen on a piece of paper, you had better give up hope at once. If you are not prepared for discouragements and disillusions, if you will not be content with a small result for a big effort, then do not begin. Lie down again and resume the uneasy doze which you call your existence.

It is very sad, is it not, very depressing and sombre? And yet I think it is rather fine, too, this necessity for the tense bracing of the will before anything worth doing can be done. I rather like it myself. I feel it to be the chief thing that differentiates me from the cat by the fire.

"Well," you say, "assume that I am braced for the battle. Assume that I have carefully weighed and comprehended your ponderous remarks; how do I begin?" Dear sir, you simply begin. There is no magic method of beginning. If a man standing on the edge of a swimming-bath and wanting to jump into the cold water should ask you, "How do I begin to jump?" you would merely reply, "Just jump. Take hold of your nerves, and jump."

As I have previously said, the chief beauty about the constant supply of time is that you cannot waste it in advance. The next year, the next day, the next hour are lying ready for you, as perfect, as unspoilt, as if you had never wasted or misapplied a single moment in all your career. Which fact is very gratifying and reassuring. You can turn over a new leaf every hour if you choose. Therefore no object is served in waiting till next week, or even until tomorrow. You may fancy that the water will be warmer next week. It won't. It will be colder.

                                                                Arnold Bennett

"That is asking a lot," you might say. Yes, but I can only repeat that time is our most precious resource. Nothing can be more rewarding at the end of our lives than a sense that we have spent more of it wisely than we have wasted.

KEY POINTS

- Never let procrastination root itself. It is a major time robber. Remember Franklin's words: 'One today is worth two tomorrows.'

- Delegation does not save the organisation's time, but it saves yours. The aim is to leave yourself free to do the work that only you can do. In practice that means delegating everything that can be delegated. But delegation is not abdication: you must establish and maintain a degree of control appropriate to the situation and the other person involved. In other words, there is an art of delegation to be mastered.

- Efficiency in the office need not be soulless. If your offices, room or desk are in good order it is like having your ship cleared for action. You can begin to work effectively.

- Meetings are essential in any form of human enterprise. But they are potential time wasters. The other person or persons present may not respect their own time as much as you have come to respect yours. It is then unlikely that they will mind wasting your time. Action is needed before, during and after a meeting to prevent this from happening. As a useful rule: always agree time limits at the outset of any meeting.

- You need to be clear about purpose, aims and objectives at work. The situation will then tell you what are your priorities in terms of importance and urgency, which are not necessarily the same thing.

> 'You cannot kill time without injuring
> eternity.'
>
> Thoreau

3. Developing a personal sense of time

'If I were asked what one thing an executive could do that would really, and quickly, make him more effective, make him achieve more and make him enjoy what he's doing. I'd say: "Make sure you know where your time goes. Don't depend on memory, it's treacherous."'

Peter Drucker's words are an invitation to adopt something akin to a scientist's approach to time management. Put time under the microscope. You cannot *manage* time that is past. But you can examine how you managed it in an objective and realistic way.

The key suggestion in this chapter is that you should keep a Time Log, a record of how you are spending your time.

I warn you in advance, from personal experience, that you could be in for a considerable shock. Yet that very shock could jolt you into action. It is like an electric charge to start up the motor of your will. You may need the amazing revelation of how much time you are wasting to steel your resolve to manage time more effectively in the future.

You may say that you already know how you spend your time. Let me repeat Drucker's words: "Don't depend on memory, it's treacherous." The experiment is still worth trying, however certain you feel. You have nothing to lose. It may confirm your impressions, or it may make you think again, to your great benefit.

The end product is not a technique, or — worse still — a complicated bureaucratic set of forms to fill in every week for the rest of your life. The exercise should be a further step towards developing a personal sense of time: where it goes and where it should be going.

A PERSONAL SENSE OF TIME

There is nothing which I wish more that you should know, and which fewer people do know, than the true use and value of time. It is in everybody's mouth, but in few people's practice. Every fool, who scatters away his whole time in nothing, utters, however, some trite commonplace sentence, of which there are millions, to prove, at once, the value and the fleetness of time. The sundials all over Europe have some ingenious inscriptions to that effect; so that nobody squanders away their time without hearing and seeing daily how necessary it is to employ well, and how irrecoverable it is if lost.

Lord Chesterfield,
Letters to His Son

Ask any ten managers or professional persons about the pressures on their time. At least nine will come up with the same sorry tales: long working hours, not meeting target dates and deadlines, fragmented days, excessive paperwork, and neglected families. A common refrain is that there aren't enough hours in the day. "I just don't know where they go," said one manager to me. He was one of the few who made the decision to find out.

KEEPING A TIME LOG

The principle of a time log or audit is to divide each day for the next week or two into fifteen-minute intervals. At the end of each hour you record how the previous hour was spent.

You can use an ordinary large desk diary — one page to a day — for the purpose. Or you can use ruled sheets of paper. Find a format that you are comfortable with. You may find the following symbols useful.

Code	Activities	Definition, if necessary	Notes
C	committees	Any pre-arranged group meeting with our without an agenda	
I	interviews	Any pre-arranged conversation, formal or informal, with a purpose	
D	discussion	Talking, not classified under C and I	
E	education	Participation in lectures, training courses, conferences and seminars	
F	figure work		
P	on the telephone		
S	dictating		
W	writing		
R	reading		
J	inspection	A personal tour of the work place, walking the job	
Q	travelling	For your work, and not doing other work listed above	
T	thinking		
O	others	Please specify what	

Fig. 3.1   *Symbols for Time Log*

You may, of course, want to amend or alter the list of prominent activities according to your trade or profession. For example, a teacher might include such headings as Lesson/lecture preparation, Marking, Teaching, Games, and Extra-curricular activities.

It takes self-discipline to get started and keep going, but once you are into the swing of it, far less time is taken up by the exercise than you might imagine. It should occupy in all no more than five minutes a day.

Even as you do it you may find that your fifteen-minute coffee break usually runs to thirty minutes. You may, for instance, have to walk to a coffee machine and queue for your turn.

Look back at the end of each week. You may be surprised at what a comparatively small percentage of your time is actually going on the top-priority tasks on your list. Time for planning, anticipating contingencies, thinking about opportunities and recharging your batteries in various ways is often conspicuously missing, squeezed out by the day-to-day overloading or slippage from other more routine activities.

If so, it is a serious matter. For a manager's effectiveness is closely related to the use he makes of time, which he needs to control, rather than the other way round, if he is to avoid constantly managing by crisis. In particular, achieving results through other people makes it essential that the leader of the working group manages his own time so that he has time to think ahead to tomorrow's problems as well as about today's decisions.

You may find that you had no idea how your time is really being spent. Memory isn't to be entirely trusted in this area because we tend to recall the productive hours of the day and to push into the background time wasted or not used to good effect. It is not unlike the old sundial inscription which reads: 'I record only the sunny hours.' The large pieces or small scraps of time taken up by matters of relatively minor importance are conveniently forgotten. These are the very items that a careful time audit should show up.

After keeping a log for three or four days, you may begin to notice opportunities for improvement. For example, you may discover that you are spending much more time than you thought possible on reading newspapers and trade journals or compiling routine reports. Could the latter be delegated? At the end of the two weeks, when the data is available, try to group your time use under key headings, such as:

ACTIVITY	HOURS SPENT	% OF TIME
1. COMMITTEES		
2. INTERVIEWS		
3. DISCUSSION		
4. EDUCATION		
5. FIGURE WORK		
6. ON THE TELEPHONE		
7. DICTATING		
8. WRITING		
9. READING		
10. INSPECTION		
11. TRAVELLING		
12. THINKING		
13. OTHERS (Specify)		

Fig. 3.2   *Summary of Time Log Data*

REVIEW AND REFLECT

After listing your findings in the above way you should carry out a rigorous review of how you are spending your time. Here is a series of questions which you should be able to answer:

● Do the time allocations reflect your priorities? Is the bulk of your time being spent on the key functions or core responsibilities of your job?

● What are the items which take up significant portions of your time and contribute nothing? What would happen if they weren't done at all?

● How much time each day was available for use at your own discretion, as opposed to being committed by other members of the organisation? Could this time be consolidated into one period rather than in small isolated pieces?

● Could any of the work be done faster or simplified without adversely affecting other parts of the organisation?

● Are you spending time on work that could be done to a satisfactory level by your subordinate or your secretary? (Look especially at constantly recurring problems, routine matters or work to do with details).

Frequently the answers to these questions show that the tasks you consider to be most important in a management or professional sense are consuming the least number of hours.

To help to correct the imbalance why not keep a daily activities log primarily in terms of goals, objectives or results rather than activities? First you need to be clear about your goals and objectives — the subject of the next three chapters.

WHAT HAPPENS TO A MANAGER'S TIME?

In recent years more than twenty studies have been made, using the diary and/or observation methods, on management work. The following is the composite picture which emerges from that research.

Managers tend to work long hours, including paperwork done at home, business meetings and social events related to business. The hours multiply in the higher echelons, but those in well-defined jobs such as accountants are likely to work shorter days. At work managers are very busy. One first-line manager attended to over 300 separate things in a day, 'resting' for only one minute in an eight-hour day. Perhaps he knew he was being watched!

Work is fragmented into brief episodes, ranging from two to nine minutes. They do not follow each other in any particular order. Problems are dealt with by quick-fire decisions. No attempt is made to assess the priorities of issues by importance: everything is equally urgent. Interruptions are the order of the day. Some executives have as much as forty telephone calls and thirty visitors in the course of a single day. Paperwork, consultations, formal meetings, inspections jostle each other in untidy profusion.

Managers at all levels spend most of their time in their own departments. Senior executives are more likely to be in their offices or in other departments than on the shopfloor. This contrasts with the practice of Japanese senior managers. When asked why he spent so much time on the shopfloor, the President of Toyota replied: "We don't make cars in my office." Most managerial communications are oral, usually face-to-face in meetings. Contacts with colleagues increase with rank. Subordinates occupy between one-third and two-thirds of a manager's time, compared to superiors who spend only a fraction of that time with him.

Planning is a key leadership function, but the research shows that few managers are skilled in this area. Uninterrupted periods of time when planning is possible are rare in the average manager's diary. Less than 5 per cent of management time goes on planning.

Lastly, research confirms that we are not very good at estimating how much time we have spent on particular activities. For example, managers tend to over-estimate the time taken up by production, paperwork, telephone calls and thinking, and to underestimate the time that goes in meetings and discussions.

These studies raise the question, "How much control can the manager have over his time?". One researcher wryly concluded: "Even had the executives wanted to change their behaviour, they did not have much chance to do so. The content of their working day is determined only to a small extent by themselves and it is difficult to change it without making considerable alterations in the organisational structure of which they are part. Before we made the study, I always thought of a chief executive as the conductor of an orchestra standing aloof on his platform. Now I am in some respects inclined to see him as the puppet in a puppet show with hundreds of people pulling the strings and forcing him to act in one way or another."

KEY POINTS

● Do not assume that you know how you are spending your time. For one or two weeks observe in detail and record how your time is spent.

● Analyse and consider the way you have organised, planned, made, used and wasted your time in the five days, and propose specific actions you intend to take to improve your efficiency in this area. For example, compare how your time is actually spent against how it ought to be spent in the light of your job description and current aims and objectives.

● Studies of managers at work confirm that most of us mismanage our time. Yet time is our scarcest resource. Unless it is managed, nothing else can be managed.

● The result of reading this chapter and making a study of how you spend your time should be a development of your personal sense of time. That sense is essential, for it must influence you throughout the working day.

> *'Go, sir, gallop, and don't forget that the world was made in six days. You can ask me for anything you like, except time.'*
> *Napoleon*

4. How To Identify Long-Term Goals

All planning is thinking forwards in time. What varies in plans is how far ahead they stretch and how precise they are. There is always a limit to how far ahead it is feasible to plan at any given time. "It is wise to look ahead," Winston Churchill once said, "but foolish to look further than you can see." Beyond a certain prospect you are really dreaming rather than thinking.

Imagine you are walking through some hills. You can see objects very clearly in the *foreground* and soon come abreast of them. There is a *middleground* which is less close, and also *far ground* — perhaps a range of higher hills. This analogy applies to life and work.

You will see that it is not possible to demarcate sharply between foreground and middleground, or middle and far grounds. They all form part of a continuum which alters in shape as you advance.

Is the foreground — the time nearest to you — a matter of seconds, minutes, hours, days or weeks? It is impossible to be dogmatic, not least because your perception of what is or is not foreground in time is influenced by circumstantial factors. For example, a sick person's foreground might drop to a matter of minutes, just as mist or blinding rain can overtake you on the hills. You can be benighted, so that your vision is reduced to a few metres ahead.

Despite these factors, the distinction between foreground,

middleground and far ground is valuable and you should train yourself to think and plan at all three ranges. Here, borrowing words from the military, I shall call those kinds of thinking *tactical, operational* and *strategic.*

This chapter aims to help you think strategically about your life and work. That presupposes an attempt on your part to look ahead, well beyond your present time commitments, to see if you can discern the shape of things to come. What is the geography you can make out on the horizon? You may want to select some features or areas (often by rejecting others) to which you will guide yourself. They can be called your *strategic goals.* Together they constitute your desired future.

LIFE PLANNING IN PERSPECTIVE

The present enthusiasm for life planning — setting strategic goals for one's life — has its origins in America. It has become widespread in Britain and elsewhere through books on time management. You should be rather cautious about accepting the concept of life planning as a mental package.

The word *goal* comes from the world of sport. Originally it meant the terminal point of a race, such as a winning-post. Now it covers both the area into which players in football and similar games attempt to drive the ball to win points and also the resulting score. In its more figurative or more general sense, a *goal* is the end towards which effort or ambition is directed.

People who love sport, such as the Americans and British, readily import analogies from sport into daily life. For example, "That isn't cricket," used to be a term of general disapproval in Britain. (Now that the relish for competitive struggle and the value placed on winning the game have invaded cricket, as all other sports, the metaphor has somewhat lost its force!).

Culturally Americans place even more value on winning than the British. They are more inclined to see life as a competitive struggle, a game with winners and losers. The great thing is to be among the winners. As President Kennedy's father drummed into him "Coming second is coming *nowhere.*"

In such a culture the first questions to ask oneself in virtually any situation are: "What is the game I am in? Where is

the goal? How are the winners distinguished from the losers?"
Goals in life tend to be competitive ones, such as to become
President or to make a million dollars within ten years. Many
strive to be President but only one secures the prize. Dollars
are scarce and sought by all. If one person has a million someone else will presumably have to make do with less. There are
winners and losers in the market-place as in politics.

Goal-setting has proved remarkably successful. For
example, when President Kennedy said that America would
put a man on the moon within ten years it was like setting a
goal for the nation. It was a competitive one, too, for the Russians could theoretically have beaten the Americans to it. That
goal was achieved admittedly at the cost of a vast amount of
human time and even vaster amounts of money. Was it all
worth it? Could those resources have been spent more fruit-
fully on other terrestrial projects?

Actually, the Russians did not try to put a man on the moon
before the Americans. Yet they were achieving other goals in
space exploration; they were competing in the game. Space
now has a military use and is a factor in the Great Game of
superpower relations. Sport and war are cousins.

The equivalent word for *goal* in the language of military
theory and practice is *objective*. Literally it is the *objective* point
towards which the advance of troops is directed. In its more
general sense of being any point aimed at, the word objective
has become one of several meaning *an end towards which effort
is directed.*

The phrase *strategic goal* combines both the metaphors of
war and sport. For *strategy* derives from the Greek words for a
'leader of an army'. Strategy is the kind of thinking and planning appropriately done by a general. It is the art of devising
plans and employing strategems towards achieving the general's ultimate objective of securing the enemy's surrender.

The sporting and military analogies (which we are hardly
conscious of as being analogies, so common and so disguised
are they in everyday speech) have much to be said in their
favour. Goals are at least clear. By setting goals or objectives,
vague aspirations are reduced into tangible and attainable
forms. But the metaphors have more force in certain areas of
life than in others. They apply especially to business enterprise
in all its forms (see the following chapter). But they don't apply

to whole sectors of your personal life. The analogies of life as
being like playing a competitive game or fighting a war or running a business soon break down.They need to be supple-
mented by other analogies.

TO LIVE IS TO JOURNEY FORWARDS

Not everyone consciously thinks of his or her life as being like a
journey, but the metaphor is deeply imbedded in Western culture. Here I should like to suggest some of the ways in which it
is a helpful metaphor when looking ahead in your life.

Suppose you are making a journey which you have planned
yourself. You can identify fairly clearly the place where you
want to be tomorrow night. Let's call that your first *objective*.
It's something tangible and immediately attainable. You can
easily identify other objectives for other nights, culminating in
the town or city where your journey ends. *End* has this convenient double meaning: end in time and end as aim or object.

For about three centuries the word *goal* has been used outside the context of sport to describe the destination of a difficult journey. It carries overtones of something attained only by
prolonged effort and hardship. If you want to get to the top of
Mount Everest or reach the South Pole you could accurately
describe these places as goals. But when you get on the local
train this morning it would not really be appropriate for you to
call your destination a few stops down the line as the *goal* of
your journey. Of course it might become a goal if the train
broke down and you had no means of travel but to walk the
next twenty miles.

The journey analogy is at least potentially free from the
limiting overtones of competition and winners/losers. You can
set objectives and goals for yourself which don't imply that you
are striving to be first. But, like all analogies, it fails to apply if
pressed too far.

For example, strictly speaking there are no maps for the
future. You can look up Mount Everest or the South Pole on
the map and decide how to get there. But there are no 'places'
that you can look up in a handbook of the future. In that respect, living is more like exploring an unknown country than
following a route on a map.

You can, however, make general assumptions about the future. Experiencing life as relative continuity as well as rapid change, people act daily upon the probability that human society will remain more-or-less the same tomorrow as it is today. In the short-term this allows you to act as if the future is predictable. For example, the position of President of the United States will be there in five years time. Therefore theoretically any senator or governor could plan to sit in the Oval Office of the White House. A whole host of careers — ready-made journeys — already exist. If you get on the right ladder or escalator in such careers you can most probably climb to a clearly-discernible top.

Scaling these social or corporate heights step by step makes sense for some people, but not for others. It is less clear that strategic goals can be set in other areas of work, let alone the rest of one's life. Did Shakespeare set himself a strategic goal of becoming the world's most famous playwright and then plan his plays accordingly? It is highly improbable that he thought that way. He may, however, have dreamt of greatness when he was a boy. As the Spanish proverb says, 'If you build no castles in the air, you build no castles anywhere'.

You can plan for part of your time but not for all of it. True, some men do make a tangible goal, like becoming President of the United States, the purpose of their lives. But this can become a strait-jacket. Moreover, when you have attained your goal what do you do next? You will have to think in wider terms than a particular goal.

KNOW YOUR VALUES

Values are essentially what you think is worthwhile (i.e. worth time) and deserving of effort. There is a reverse effect. If you spend time and energy on something or someone you will value the object more than one which demands from you nothing. To some extent, by choosing an object and devoting ourselves to it, we create value.

In the context of time management values have potentially a most important role to play. They are stars by which you can navigate. You will not succeed in touching them with your hands, but like the seafarer or desert traveller you choose them as guides, and, following them, you reach your destination. Navigational skill is especially important at times when your future — for one reason or another — resembles more an uncharted sea than the next stretch of a familiar river.

Values play this critical part in directing your course whether you are conscious of them or not. The first step towards better navigational skill is to become more aware of the values which are presently influencing your life choices now.

Peter Larking at first enjoyed his work as marketing director of a large cosmetic company. He liked the social life and the high salary he earned; he travelled all over the world staying in expensive hotels. But it was a burning ambition to head the multi-national parent company which drove him to work all hours of the day and night. The weekends he spent thinking solely about business or on the telephone to colleagues or customers. At 56 years, the year he gained a seat on the main Board, his wife divorced him and he had his second ulcer. Next year he had a coronary, and he had to give up on doctor's advice his sole remaining pleasure of mountain climbing. Just before he was 58 he was so busy managing a takeover bid which — if successful — would almost certainly secure him the coveted job of Chief Executive, that he did not have time to visit his eighteen year old son in hospital who had contracted a serious illness. The day after Peter got the top job his son died. "Although I never had much time to spend with the boy," he said to his secretary, "he was the most important thing in the world to me." Was he?

This cautionary tale is a reminder to know your values and to keep them in sight. Let other people question them if it serves to make you think more about them.

Know your values and adhere to them. But don't make the mistake of imposing them on others. Remember what William James wrote: 'The first thing to learn in intercourse with others is non-interference with their own particular ways of being happy, provided that those ways are not assumed to interfere by violence with ours.'

A ZEST FOR LIVING

If you want to enjoy one of the greatest luxuries in life, the luxury of having enough time, time to rest, time to think things through, time to get things done and know you have done them to the best of your ability, remember there is only one way. Take enough time to think and plan things in the order of their importance. Your life will take a new zest, you will add years to your life, and more life to your years. Let all your things have their places. Let each part of your business have its time.

Benjamin Franklin

Values can be expressed in the language of purpose, and statements of purpose can in turn be understood in terms of values. For example, if you make self-fulfilment your number one priority in life, that may reveal that for you the value of the individual comes first. If the self-fulfilment of other individuals is what matters, well and good. If it is *your* self-fulfilment that counts, at the expense of others, then you may end up like Dr. Samuel Johnson's acquaintance — 'a lover of himself, without a rival.'

THE NATURE OF POLICY

Sometimes it is impossible to identify clearly a strategic goal. Then purposeful activity may be a matter of seeking to better your competitive position, like a general securing the commanding heights. You can improve your strategic capability. Even when you do not know precisely where you are going some sort of forward movement is usually possible and may produce unexpected results. Columbus set out to find India but discovered America instead.

Alongside strategies and tactics of various kinds — the means you employ to achieve ends — must be placed *policies* and *routines*. What is their relation to time management? Routines will be discussed in the next chapter, so let us focus here upon policy.

A policy is essentially a decision of principle. It can help you to make choices when you face the need for them. You may have a policy of taking your holidays in the spring or autumn, rather than summer. That is not an invariable rule but a guideline. It saves you time because you don't have to think each year from scratch.

Policy-making is clearly important, whether it is done by an individual or by the leaders of a corporate body. To repeat the point, it is not the same as a strategy, although it may be related to it. Your policies are a body of principles that guide action.

Looking upon policies in this way prevents them from becoming settled courses of action, definite procedures or routines. No one case is the same. The value of having policies, however, in the context of this book stems from the fact that decision-making is a time-consuming activity. If you can cut down time spent in agonising over every problem by making some generic decisions it will set you free.

A policy is not the same as a rule. For example, a company may announce that its rule is not to give or receive bribes. Theoretically there is always the possibility of an exception but no exceptions are envisaged. A policy is a guide rather than a rule. It implies that the person applying it will use discretion and judgement.

Policies like rules should be absolutely clear, since their prime purpose is to prevent confusion and time wasting. A policy does not last forever. When in doubt it must be reviewed. When outdated or shown to be wrong it must be changed. If it is changed too often, then it fails to serve its purpose and actually causes confusion and wastes time. Order — counter-order — disorder.

KEY POINTS

● The comparison of life to a journey is a powerful metaphor. Seeing your life in this way can be a positive help.

● Some journeys have objectives and routes; others are explorations into the unknown.

● Policy is not the same as strategy. You may be able to make progress without a strategy. When you encounter obstacles, problems or crises it is useful to have some clear policies as guides.

● A sense of purpose and a sense of direction can be developed. They come from the mental effort of trying to identify at least some strategic goals and then pursuing them energetically. You can always modify or change them in the light of experience.

● Know your values, for they govern the direction and the manner in which you spend your time. Review them annually, setting aside some time to do so. Imagine them as the stars by which you are navigating the ship of your life.

● Don't interfere unnecessarily with the values of others. 'God knows well who are the best pilgrims.'

> *'If you do not know where you are going you can take any road.'*

5. How to Make Middle-term Plans

Operational plans function on the middleground of your life or your organisation. In military terms, strategy is the concern of generals and tactics of colonels and below. Operational plans, coming in between, are the responsibility of divisional and brigade commanders.

What counts as the area of future time and activity subject to operational plans will vary widely. For you the middleground may be the next three or four months, or a year or two at the most, while for a giant oil company or an international bank it could be much longer. Choose the length of time that suits you. Quarters of a year may suit you for progress review purposes, but not for forward planning. However you define the middleground it will always merge into more distant time. For the purpose of this chapter I shall assume your middleground is from one to twelve months.

As a principle, the further away in time things are, the less definite they are perceived to be. There are instruments, such as telescopes, which qualify this natural law in regard to space, but there is not a 'time machine' for the future. Operational planning concerns that stretch of the future which is neither immediately near to you nor distant from you. Therefore, it will be fairly definite but not completely so.

Which should come first, strategic or operational planning of your use of time (along with the energy, talents and money available to you)? It doesn't really matter. Logically, of course, strategic thinking should be your priority. For if you do not know what point you are making for in the distant hills, it may be puzzling to know which route to take in the middleground. But, leaving the analogy for a moment, engaging energetically in setting operational goals and objectives may lead on to the more distant future. In other words, a strategy may emerge from what is strictly speaking operational thinking. It is as if you can think either deductively or inductively about the future: ranging from the general to the particular, or the particular to the general. In some circumstances operational thinking may be the only option open to you. If so, start there.

TIME BUDGETING

Efficiency, it has been said, is doing things right, while effectiveness is doing the right things. But how do you know what are the *right* things to be doing with your time?

Clearly the first task is to sit back and ask yourself such questions as, "What are my key goals and objectives in the next three months? What is it important for me to accomplish, progress or initiate? How should my life and work be different in a year's time from what it is now?"

Obviously the content of your answers will be unique to you. Here are some suggestions about the way to think clearly, so that the results of your operational planning meet the necessary criteria if they are to be implemented effectively. You have to compose the tunes, but I can tell you how to write music that orchestras can play.

Let us begin with the most difficult bit of all — sitting back. The object of moving your chair back is so that you can see a broader picture. Those preoccupied with day-to-day work often develop a form of tunnel vision. They cannot see the wood for the trees. For them the act of sitting back must be deliberate. It must be repeated time and time again, until it becomes second nature.

Imagine that your mind has two lenses, like a camera. The wide-angle lens allows you to see the wider picture of the middleground, while your telescopic lens should enable you to focus upon a particular area of it in some detail.

You would see both a wider picture and further ahead if you could climb on to higher ground or be lifted up in a helicopter.

Imagine yourself in a helicopter viewing the next six months. From this height the main feature should stand out in bold relief.

In the 1960s Shell identified this *helicopter vision* as a core ingredient of success in its senior managers. Whether you are self-employed or work for an organisation, you should develop this ability.

QUALITY	DEFINITION
Imagination	The ability and drive to discern the various useful possibilities and alternatives which are inherent in a problem, but which are not obvious to less perceptive observers.

Sense of Reality	The extent to which:
	    An individual's interpretation of which action has to be taken shows that full account has been taken of the realities of the situation.
	    An individual displays an almost instinctive feeling or intuition for the right course of action.

Power of Analysis	The ability and drive to:
	    Transform, break down or reformulate an apparently complicated problem into workable terms.
	    Continue the analysis of the problem until all the relevant aspects have been thoroughly and critically examined.

Helicopter Vision	The ability and drive to:
	    Look at problems from a higher vantage point with simultaneous attention to relevant details.
	    Place facts and problems within a broader context by immediately detecting relationships with systems of wider scope.
	    Shape one's work accordingly on the basis of a personal vision.

Fig. 5.1   *Shell Managers — Valued Qualities*

Reserve time for wide-angle planning. As the research studies in Chapter Two suggested, planning is often and easily squeezed out from an ineffective manager's day. It doesn't demand your attention. But don't neglect it. Invest time in thinking and planning ahead and it will pay you handsome dividends. Put some dates and times for it down in your diary now.

It is often useful to go away for a day or two with your associates or team for this exercise. Being in different physical surroundings can have the psychological effect of distancing you from your everyday life, giving you a new perspective.

WHAT AN OPERATIONAL PLAN SHOULD DO FOR YOU

Essentially an operational plan should show you and others a limited but feasible number of goals and objectives, together with plans for achieving them.

In a given calendar period, assuming you are not starting from scratch, a group of objectives/plans will be in various stages of completion. It is like managing a portfolio of shares, each with its particular contribution and level of performance.

The plan proper should detail exactly what steps have to be taken to complete the task. When you have thought forwards try thinking back from the end as well. This will help you to avoid leaving out essential steps.

A good plan will always answer the questions: Who? When? Where? How? What? and Why? If you are in doubt — or even if you are not in doubt — it is wise to check plans with someone else. You may be making some unconscious assumptions which another person will swiftly spot. Two heads are better than one.

What an operational plan will not do for you is make anything happen. It is no more than an architect's blueprint. If you are only an architect and not a builder, nothing will happen.

On the other hand, a good operational plan will save you time — lots of it. Remember, research studies confirm what common sense tells you: the more time spent planning a project, the less total time is required for it. Imagine two groups tackling the same common task. Group A skimps on planning: the leader is action-centred in the wrong sense of that phrase — he regards thinking as a waste of time. As a consequence Group A takes a long time to complete the task. For example, nobody is clear on the objective; alternative courses of action have not been explored.

By contrast. Group B takes adequate time to plan. The objective is made clear and definite; time limits and other boundaries are clarified. The optimum course of action or solution is chosen from a list of feasible options. There may even have been a brain-storming session to generate creative ideas. Everyone feels committed. The job gets done faster.

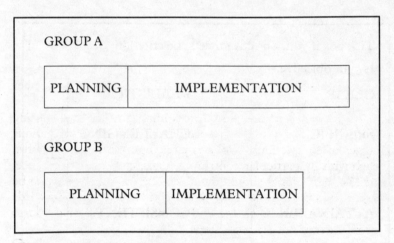

Fig. 5.2   *Planning/Implementation Ratio*

A casual observer in the planning phase may have given marks to the leader of Group A for decisiveness. But looking at the exercise overall it is clear who made the better decisions.

The principle that planning saves time applies at the strategic, operational and tactical levels. Always work on this key principle that "Every moment spent planning saves three or four in execution."

CHARACTERISTICS OF GOALS AND OBJECTIVES

To summarize earlier points: goals and objectives are words drawn from the sportsfield and the battlefield respectively. They should be definite in the sense of being well defined. Objectives are tangible and near at hand (the archery target provides another analogy). Goals may imply more distance or greater difficulty.

Assuming that a page or two ago you identified at least one objective for the next six months of your life or work, now check it against the following criteria.

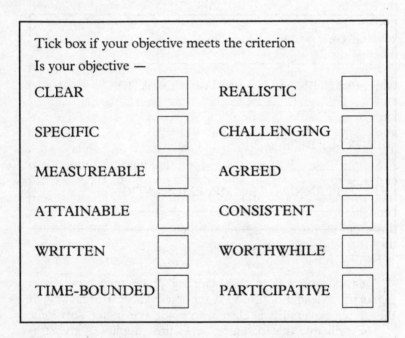

Tick box if your objective meets the criterion

Is your objective —

CLEAR ☐	REALISTIC ☐
SPECIFIC ☐	CHALLENGING ☐
MEASUREABLE ☐	AGREED ☐
ATTAINABLE ☐	CONSISTENT ☐
WRITTEN ☐	WORTHWHILE ☐
TIME-BOUNDED ☐	PARTICIPATIVE ☐

Fig. 5.3   *Checklist — Hallmarks of Good Objectives*

You may not have ticked all the boxes. This may not matter. For example, some objectives can only be measured by judgement rather than by quantitative methods, and you may hesitate to tick MEASURABLE. If you are setting a personal objective — such as to compete in a marathon and complete

the course within the top half of the field — then PARTICI-
PATIVE may not be relevant. There should, however, be a lot
of ticks. Otherwise your objective is too vague and you are dealing in hopes rather than plans.

TIME NORMS FOR ROUTINE ACTIVITIES

When thinking ahead about our lives or work the centrepiece
will tend to be goals and objectives. For example, a manager
may want promotion to the next grade or to buy a new house.
His corporate objectives, in the next six months for instance,
may include the successful launch of a new product in the
north-east. But in the background are the continuing activities
which cannot be described as goal-seeking without artificiality.
They are usually lumped under the heading of *routine*.

From the French *route*, a travelled way, routine means an established course of procedure, something you do habitually
and regularly. It is like the road leading to your house: you
know it so well that you do not have to think about such things
as direction as you drive down it. Therefore it is a less interesting road than the unknown road you explore on holiday.

Simply because they are so commonplace, routines can
easily be overlooked in time management. As they become
more mechanical, inflexible and uninspired, routines may also
become more time consuming. If so, they cease to be worth the
time allowed for them. Moreover, being more-or-less habitual,
they tend to escape close scrutiny.

Before your next operational planning session, try to identify
some of these established and recurring activities, using the
table below to chart them. It may be worth holding them up to
the touchstones of purpose and aims, goals and objectives. You
or your staff can prepare for this review by keeping track of
how much time these tasks normally take. If necessary, break
them down into measurable parts using work-study methods.
Then assign a realistic norm — the amount of time you think
the task should take. This approach will:

● Highlight any routine activity that seems to be consuming a
   disproportionate amount of time. If it is something you are
   doing yourself and you have others working under you,

consider delegating some or all of it. You may want to
question why it is being done at all.

● Assist in replanning your work. For any major deviation
from the time norm will suggest a need for time management action.

● Prevent the application of Parkinson's Law — that work
expands to fill the time available for it.

ACTIVITY OR PROCEDURE	TIME NORM

Fig. 5.4   *Time Norms*

Time norms for routine tasks can be seen as challenges.
Indeed by setting time norms for these regular courses or procedures, you are beginning to turn them into an objective.

You can build on this idea by introducing success criteria to
inoculate against the deadening effects of routine: mechanical,
uninspired and inflexible driving down well-travelled roads.

THE QUARTERLY REVIEW

At 3, 4 or 6 monthly intervals (whichever suits your situation) you should carry out a progress review. Look upon it as a learning experience, for you can only master the skills of time planning by practice. But practice without subsequent reflection matching it against theory or principles is useless.

Look in particular at objectives you failed to achieve in the period under review. What went wrong? There are four possible causes, listed in the table below. Avoid blaming external circumstances too much: it can become a habit. People often rationalize failures due to their own shortcomings by blaming factors which they assume, claim or pretend were outside their dominion.

Circumstances beyond your control	Could you not have foreseen these circumstances 4 or 6 months ago? What indicators did you ignore?
Circumstances within your control	Were there factors within your control, such as recruiting enough staff, which you ignored or performed badly? Did the failure lie within your powers as an implementer rather than planner?
Insufficient motivation	Did you write down 4 or 6 months ago some objectives that you had no real intention of completing? Goals are demanding: did the difficulty involved reveal your lack of motivation?
Insufficient skill in setting objectives	Review the actual goals or objectives against the 12 criteria in Fig. 5.3. Did the lack of a deadline, for example, explain why the job was not done on time?

Fig. 5.5   *Diagnosing Causes of Limited Success*

If you have been thinking strategically during the period under review you may well have abandoned or altered an objective for a perfectly good reason. Perhaps a more strategically important opportunity suddenly opened up, or a genuine obstacle in your path caused you to alter course. Planning should always have contingency provisions. Uncommitted resources, if only some of your own time, should be kept in reserve. Unexpected opportunities and problems, even crises, are part-and-parcel of life. A wise manager plans with such pleasant or unpleasant contingencies in mind. As an Israeli general once said, "A plan is a very good basis for changing your mind."

SUMMARY

- Develop your helicopter vision — the skills of taking a broader and longer look at the work you are doing. Set it in strategic context and identify key operational goals and objectives.

- A plan gives you something to work on. But it is only half the battle. The other half is to implement it. Remember that planning saves time by cutting down time needed for execution.

- Goals and objectives should not be vague. There is an art in setting them for yourself or others. Like silver the genuine article should bear certain hallmarks, such as being specific, measurable and subject to a deadline.

- You can only learn how to set objectives by setting them and by reviewing performance afterwards. In the case of limited success thinking backwards after the expiry date should enable you to identify which of the four causes in Fig. 5.5 led to failure. Don't make the same mistake three times.

- Stay flexible, especially over the means by which you plan to achieve the objective. Change objectives more slowly, and then only if a better opportunity arises or external factors really compel you to do so.

*'If you want something to happen you must
make time and space for it.'*

6. Planning The Day

"After all your years of experience in management, do you have a golden rule for managers?" This question was put to Peter Drucker at a London conference.

"I have no experience in management but I have seen a lot of managers as an outsider," replied Drucker. "One golden rule is to ask yourself if you know what you are being paid to do — and do not believe the answer is work. What are the two or three things which, if you really perform, will make a difference? If you do this, the rest easily takes care of itself."

Strategical and operational planning, the subjects of the last two chapters, should have provided you with an answer to Drucker's question. Within a framework of clear, ordered and truthful thinking about yourself and your future you should now be able to get down to the tactical level of 'telescopic lens' focus of planning with real confidence.

This chapter is about how to plan effectively the time that is immediately available to you — today. A day is a natural unit of time. As yesterday is gone and tomorrow is yet to be, it follows that today must be centre stage in tactical time management.

ATTITUDES TO TIME

Before plunging into the practicalities of daily time management it is worth asking yourself each morning: "Do I intend to live in the present today?" For it is actually sometimes quite difficult to live fully in the present. Sometimes, for what seems a perfectly good reason, yesterday or tomorrow attracts us far more than today.

Here is another possible issue for your fundamental thinking programme. What is your philosophy about the value of today, as compared to tomorrow or yesterday? Does your philosophy help you to give yourself to the demands and joys, disappointments and opportunities, of today?

Sometimes people resolve the matter by saying that today alone is real. But you cannot be sure of that. In some sense yesterday is still real and tomorrow may be as well. If you define reality as what you can see or touch, or experience in the present, you reduce its meaning. Reality is partly a human value judgement. If you value tomorrow more than today it may indeed be more real to you.

Escapism is consciously or unconsciously diverting your mind to purely imaginary activity or entertainment to escape from the realities or routines of today. You can also escape from today by living imaginatively in the past or the future. Of course escapism in itself is not necessarily good or bad: we are all escapists on occasion, not least because our minds need refreshment and recreation as well as our bodies. But habitual escapism is another matter: it militates against any form of managing your time well.

Philosophy and religion are partly about freeing people to live today. Faith can deliver from care or anxiety about tomorrow and regret or guilt about yesterday. It can engineer in us a valuable attitude to the past, based on gratitude. So we can remember the past without reliving it each day. There can grow in us an attitude of hope towards the future which is not quite the same as optimism.

Experiencing that ideal of living one hundred per cent in the present minute, incidentally, is sometimes literally marvellous. To be totally absorbed in what you are doing is a mystical experience in its own right.

Most of us fall short of this ideal. This is necessarily so, because today is framed by yesterday and tomorrow, just as this minute or hour is framed — given meaning — by its context of the time before and after. It is human for us 'to look behind and before, and pine for what is not'. The problem is one of balance more than anything else. The previous two chapters have been concerned with looking ahead to the far ground and middleground of the probable future. Both individuals in their working lives and corporate enterprises need to imagine and to plan realistically where and what they want to be in, say, five years time, and then again over shorter periods such as the next three months. Part of today's meaning or significance must come from its place in that scheme of things. But today has its own autonomy.

I see now that today is both the aftermath of all my yesterdays and the prelude to all my tomorrows. It is the time when, if I choose to do so, I can reflect and review the past, my own or the past in some more general sense. It is the time when I can think forwards and try to identify the stars by which to direct my course in the future. But it is also a day in its own right, with a unique set of people, demands, duties, opportunities, hopes and fears. Some of these may link up with the future and some may not. It is part of the fun that I have no means of telling, except perhaps the occasional flash of insight or the promptings of intuition. Only at some future date, when I look back, will I be able to see what was significant or not.

From these reflections, if you agree with the conclusion, you can see our attention should be gently and firmly directed on to today. Like a lobster in a pot, it is difficult for you to go backwards in time. As for the future, it still awaits creation. Today's work well done remains your best preparation for it. And to do work that builds on yesterday's and prepares for tomorrow, you need to budget your time for each day with care.

As a personal policy, I suggest that thinking directly about the future or the past should occupy no more than ten per cent of your time a day. Days which you have set aside for planning or review will be obvious exceptions to that rule.

BEGINNING WITH THE YEAR'S DIARY

Diaries are essential tools for time planners. Few things should give you more pleasure than the gift of next year's diary: all those empty pages, the promise of another year of life.

The shape or form of your diary is mostly a matter of personal choice. Many people prefer a combination of a large desk diary — a page per day — which lives in the office and is used also by their secretaries — together with a pocket diary. It is essential, of course, to keep these synchronized, otherwise you will be accepting invitations to meetings on the morning when your secretary says you are free for something else. (You may adopt the system that generally she may make provisional bookings only for you at times other than when you have given her discretion to fix meetings she knows you want to happen).

Various commercial time management diaries are now on the market. Some offer an 18 month or two-year 'time planner' chart, which is useful if you book that far ahead. It is wise to have a policy as to how far ahead you are prepared to commit yourself, incidentally. As a principle, keep your options open as long as possible. Don't commit your time too far ahead unless you are sure it's right for you to do so. Committing time in this way, like writing cheques, is easily done, but can be painful when the day of settlement arrives.

Personally, I find a diary system that I can assemble myself, such as the excellent Filofax system (see Appendix B), most useful. In a loose-leaf leather notebook you can clip in the diary of your choice, and a selection of other useful pages. You can also keep some notes on your key aims and objectives under the same cover as your calendar diary: a valuable reminder that they belong together. A disadvantage for some people would be that the larger sizes of Filofax binders do not fit comfortably into pockets or handbags.

PLANNING THE DAY

He who every morning plans the transactions of the day and follows out that plan carries a thread that will guide him through the labyrinth of the most busy life. The orderly arrangement of his time is like a ray of light which darts itself through all his occupations. But where no plan is laid, where the disposal of time is surrendered merely to the chance of incidents, chaos will soon reign.

Victor Hugo

Having obtained next year's diary, block out holidays, family dates, and non-work events, such as meetings of local committees or councils of which you are a member. These are your committed times. Make sure you transfer all your work commitments into the new diary as well. Add in any important deadlines by which activities have to be completed.

Suddenly, the blank year begins to look rather full. There is still plenty of uncommitted time, however, and managing that well must be your principal priority.

THE DAILY LIST

It is an essential discipline to compile a programme for the day. Make out a fresh list of what you have on and also what you want to achieve in the free time available. Don't rely solely on your diary entries; they do not cover your day; add them into your list. Later, with experience, you may be able to make the list mentally, using your diary as a memory aid or using a written list only on complicated days.

Set time limits for all tasks. Get into the way of always estimating the amount of time required to do each job, such as conducting an interview or writing a report. Check afterwards to see if your estimate was realistic.

Then establish your priorities. A priority is composed of two elements in various mixtures: *urgency* and *importance*. It is urgent that you have a punctured tyre on your car repaired, but it is not important. It is important that you begin to think about next year's marketing strategy but it is not urgent. But it is both urgent and important that you convince the chief executive at your meeting with him at 4.30 p.m. about new sales campaigns.

Some tasks that lack importance and urgency may be worth achieving first. The time/benefit ratio can be a good guide here. If the benefit is substantial and the time taken is small, do it. For example, before you can settle down to an important item, such as composing a letter to your chief client with a proposition, there may be a couple of minor tasks you can delegate. Your use of a few minutes to assign the tasks gives those concerned more notice and makes more sense.

Some people find it useful to have a system of letters,

numbers or stars to make the various orders of priority. A letter system, for example, might include:

A   MUST be done today
B   SHOULD be done today
C   MIGHT be done today

Probably you will not reach the bottom of your A and B lists, but do not let that bother you. If you have worked according to your sense of priorities you will have done the important jobs, and that is what managing your time at work is about.

Planning your day should not be done in a few minutes on the back of an envelope. Budget a reasonable time for your daily planning. Some people like to do it at the beginning of the day's work. Others prefer to plan their day the night before. This has the advantage that you can sleep on it. Sometimes after a night's rest other points for your list will occur to you or you may alter your priorities. Your subconscious mind will often suggest these alterations like a computer doing its work for you.

Check through your planned day to see if there are any gaps, any pieces of marginal time, that can be filled or put to good use. As Friedrich Nietzsche said, "When one has much to put into them, a day has a hundred pockets." You are more likely to fill the spare pockets if you identify them in advance and allocate some tasks — such as writing a letter or making a telephone call — to them.

One word of caution: if you find yourself transferring an item on your list from one day to another, it may be a sign that you are procrastinating. Scrutinize it carefully to ensure that this is not the case.

Remember also to remain flexible. Someone — such as a family member or important customer — may put in a claim on your time and they may deserve a higher priority than the next item on your list.

What matters most now? That is the question you should be asking yourself constantly throughout the day. The answers must be related to constantly changing circumstances and the needs of the minute, yet they must not be mutually self-defeating in the longer-term. It is essentially a series of value judgements, requiring from you a rare measure of mental discipline in the service of an unerring sense of time.

VALUABLE ADVICE

Charles M. Schwab, who transformed Bethlehem Steel Company into the largest independent steel producer in the world, once issued a challenge over the dinner table to a management consultant named Ivy Lee: "Show me a way to get more things done with my time and I'll pay you any fee within reason." Lee handed him a pad of blank paper. "Each evening write down the things you have to do tomorrow," he said, "and number them in order of importance. First thing in the morning start working on item one and continue with it until you have finished. Then start on item two ... then the same with three ... then four. Don't be worried if you haven't finished them all. If you can't do it by this method you can't do it by any other. Use this system every day."

Shortly afterwards Schwab sent Lee a cheque for $25,000. He said later that it was the most profitable lesson he had ever learnt in his business career.

This practice of spending the last few minutes of each working day preparing your list for the next morning has much to commend it. Successful managers have mentioned this more frequently than anything else as an aid to effective time management. If postponed until the morning, list preparation is often done in a hurried or perfunctory way as other activities begin to press on your time. The urgent items then tend to dominate, completely eclipsing the important items that should be in places number one, two or three.

If you find that your daily planning is not working very well, ask yourself first "Am I at least achieving my highest priorities?" If the answer is "No" or "Doubtful — some of the time only," you should work through the following checklist of questions:

● Are you trying to accomplish too much in a day?

● Did some tasks not get done because you were not ready at that time to do them?

● Was the item or task clearly formulated?

● Do you find it difficult to make decisions?

● Did you have all the available information?

● Had you neglected to plan sufficiently for the day because you were feeling under pressure?

● Did you abandon the task because it was too difficult or too boring?

● Was lack of self-confidence at the root of the failure?

A review of this kind can establish whether or not your time budget was realistic in the first place. If it was realistic, then the problem lies in the area of execution.

The most common reason given to me by managers for failing to accomplish what they set out to do is summarized in one word — interruptions. There are good and not-so-good interruptions. Sometimes, as for a doctor on call in the middle of the night, an interruption is merely a summons to do the job we are paid for doing. Other potential interruptions are more like contrary winds pushing us off course. To counter them, you must learn to use one of the shortest and most time-saving words in the English language — "No."

LEARN TO SAY NO

Effectiveness at work depends upon knowing what *not* to do. Over-commitment is a sure road to failure. It can lead to a breakdown in your health.

Sue Townsend, author of two best-selling Adrian Mole books, had a heart attack at the age of forty. "I had become something of a workaholic without realizing it," she confessed. "I did everything anyone asked me to do. I suppose it's a form of insecurity, but I've never been able to say 'No.' Since my heart attack I have improved and I usually insist on sleeping on any proposal, often before turning it down."

You may find it hard to refuse someone's request for your time. Possibly you feel that the other person will think less of you for doing so. Learn to decline with tact and firmness.

Don't misunderstand me; I'm not counselling you against helping people. I'm talking about the times when you say yes when in your heart you know it should have been no. For you could have put that time to better use.

When you say no, if possible say it promptly. Thus you will avoid raising false hopes only to be dashed later. Such vague phrases as "Let me think about it" or "I don't know" — do breed an expectancy. Of course, if you are in genuine doubt by all means play for time. Ask for more information, perhaps in the form of a written request with background data.

Remember that you do have the right to say no. Although it is normally courteous to give a reason, even an invented one, you do not have to excuse yourself every time you turn down a request. Politeness is never out of place. Be sensitive as well; you may think you have more important matters to attend to, but the other person may have different ideas. What is important and what is not depends to some extent upon where you are sitting.

THE TIME FANATIC

You are now growing more enthusiastic and becoming more skilled in daily time management. That puts you at risk of becoming a time fanatic. Arnold Bennett warned his readers against "the terrible danger of becoming that most odious and least supportable of persons — a prig". He defined a prig as "a tedious individual who, having made a discovery, is so impressed by his discovery that he is capable of being gravely displeased because the entire world is not also impressed by it."

Therefore, when you set out on the enterprise of using all your time, it is just as well to remind yourself that your own time, and not other people's time, is the material with which you have to work. The world turned on its axis before you began to budget your time, and will continue to roll on regardless of what you do with your day. Refrain from talking too much about your new enthusiasm or overacting the part of time manager. Avoid telling your wife and children, your boss or subordinate, how much time they are wasting each day. You will find ultimately that managing your own time is all you can do.

Another danger is being tied to your programme like a dog to a post. A daily list is a good servant but a bad master. Your daily to-do list of priorities should be respected but not canonised into holy writ. It is a tool to be used, not an idol for worship. "To treat one's programme with exactly the right amount of deference, to live with not too much and not too little elasticity is scarcely the simple affair it may appear to the inexperienced," concludes Arnold Bennett.

The 'List' can become like a tyrant in people's lives, be they chief executives or housewives. The following passage, by Cambridge historian Dr. Jonathan Steinberg, should help to inoculate you against the danger of becoming a complete time management fanatic:

'The unexpected caller, pleasant or unpleasant, disturbs the pattern of your time. That time is already allotted. Hence there is no time to help somebody who needs it, to relax and enjoy a chat on the street.

Enjoyment is always for *after* when all the jobs with deadlines, the letters to be answered, the calls to be made, have been despatched. But that time never comes. There are always more letters, deadlines, jobs and so life gets postponed until an indefinite *after* — until it is too late. A hamster on a treadmill has about the same sort of freedom.'

Using time effectively should always be your ideal but it should never become an obsession. If your values are right it never will. Remember always the end for which time is being managed. If a superior end appears, be flexible. One of the aims of daily time management is precisely to be free in this way: to have time to spare for the unexpected. That entails doing what needs to be done in the most economical way. When you are not fishing, mend your nets.

KEY POINTS

- Tactical planning focuses upon the immediate time available to you, which is measured out in days.

- Check your attitude to the present, for without concentrating on today (at the expense of thinking about yesterday or tomorrow) you will achieve nothing.

- Make out a list of what you want to do each day — a shopping list of items arranged or marked in some order of priority. Do it the evening before, so that you can sleep on it.

- Review each day briefly, identifying the successes, analysing the reasons for the failures. Avoid making excuses for yourself to yourself; dig down for the real reasons.

- Learn to say no, otherwise you will become merely the servant to the priorities of others.

- It is not easy to become efficient without being odious. Your practice of time management should enable you to contribute more to society and to others, not act as their judge.

- Do not become a slave to your planned daily programme. The aim is to free yourself from time pressures in order to work and to live more rewardingly. There's always time for important things. If something is important, you'll make time for it. Try always to enjoy whatever you are doing, and don't waste time regretting what you don't make time to do.

> *'It's not enough to be busy. The question is:*
> *What are you busy about?'*
>
> *Henry Thoreau*

7. Making Best Use Of Your Best Time

The quality of time matters more than the quantity of time. Therefore what could be called quality control of your time should be a matter of absorbing interest to you. The chief principle here is to make the best use of your best time.

The first aim of this chapter is to make you aware of what is your best or naturally high-quality time, so that you can employ it for high-quality work. As work of this nature will almost certainly involve thinking in some form or another, the second aim of the chapter is to remind you of how to use your brain effectively.

You may feel that you know yourself pretty well. But research suggests, rather surprisingly, that most managers either cannot identify the hours when they are naturally more mentally active or do not plan their time with this factor in mind. Therefore high-quality time is often partially wasted on low-quality activities.

Mary Stannard's husband was made redundant by an American pharmaceutical company where he had been a sales manager. Nothing suitable came up in the way of a job, and after a year he and Mary decided to invest the redundancy money by buying a corner shop in Farnham. Some time before Mary had discovered she had a real interest and talent for becoming a journalist. But she had left her secretarial job when the children were born and never followed it up. Now Mary resolved that after she had sent the children to school, done the housework, helped her husband in the shop, filled in the daily accounts and looked after her ageing mother who lived nearby, she would really get down to some writing. After all, they now needed some extra income. "I'll help," volunteered her husband. "I'll put the children to bed and cook supper every night." But by five, when Mary finally got out her typewriter, she was too tired even to think. What should she do?

WHAT IS YOUR BEST TIME?

Essentially it is the time when you do your best work. You can discover it by the process of experiment. Maybe for you it's early in the morning, perhaps in the afternoon or late in the evening. For example, Winston Churchill used to work best late at night and in the early hours of the morning. He did not get up before breakfast; instead he stayed in bed most of the morning reading papers, dictating letters or seeing people.

Some people concentrate best around lunch time or later in the afternoon, but they are fairly exceptional. The major division comes between Larks and Night Owls. Some research suggests that more introverted and ambiverted people tend to be Larks while extroverts tend to be Night Owls. Does this apply to you?

For the majority of us, then, any task requiring solitude, concentration and creative thinking is best done before 10.00 a.m. You can accomplish more with less effort if you programme important items at this high performance time. You may be one of the minority who do creative work best at night or in the afternoon. If so, develop a strategy based upon using your prime time for creative thinking or strategically significant pieces of work.

A friend of Mary Stannard, who had read about the principle of making best use of your best time, suggested she should postpone such chores as housework and bookkeeping to the afternoon, and contract with her husband to help him in the shop only before lunch and closing time, when there were many people in the shop. By getting up for an hour before breakfast and writing for two hours between 9.30 and 11.30, she found her solution. "Actually I can do five hours work in those three hours", she told her husband after the first week. A year later she had become a part-time reporter for the local newspaper and a regular contributor to various national journals.

Why do most people think best early in the morning? Consider the relation between mental and physical fatigue. A manager who has completed a long, hard day's work arrives home suffering from mental fatigue. His eyes and face-muscles feel tired; he is irritable; he avoids more mental work and finds it hard to make decisions. If he does have to make decisions whilst in this state the quality will be suspect. He wants to relax, yet thoughts keep crowding in on his mind. The remedy for such mental fatigue is not more work but recreation, outdoor exercise or any activity which holds his interest without making demands on his brain.

The man who has been digging trenches or the woman who has been coping with children and housework all day suffers from mainly physical fatigue. Muscles are tired; bodies feel heavy. It's an effort to think. He or she needs a good sit down and something to replace the blood sugar that has been used up. In extreme cases he or she needs complete relaxation and sleep. Often physical and mental fatigue go together.

Some years ago an experiment was carried out to measure mental fatigue. A man was given a number of arithmetical problems consisting of the mental multiplication of two sets of four figure numbers. Starting at 11.00 a.m. he continued without a break until 11.00 p.m. He completed 67 sums. The time taken for each problem increased from five minutes for the first to about ten minutes for the last. That was due, quite understandably to fatigue.

A different man was set the same test starting at 11.00 p.m. after a hard day at work. For the first 20 problems he did as well as the other, taking about an hour and a half. Then he went to pieces, taking up to 25 minutes for a single problem. Clearly an additional factor which had come into play.

In human life there is a natural rhythm of getting up some time after dawn and going to bed some time after sunset. This rhythm is extremely hard to break; even after long spells of night shift and day sleeping a man will show proneness to fatigue in approximately the following proportions.

Fig. 7.1   *Energy Curve*

Even when you have been awake all night you will feel a new onrush of energy just as dawn breaks. The pattern and insistence of this rhythm varies with individual temperaments, with habit and with climate. But it affects most of us so strongly that in normal conditions it is a good policy to programme creative or demanding work when your energy level is rising, before or after breakfast. The morning is the time for hard work. Put *interesting* work — certain meetings or social events — in your off-peak time to give yourself some extra stimulation.

Remember it is more time economical to remedy fatigue before it becomes acute. The less fatigue the shorter the rest to restore you to full efficiency. It is better to part-exchange your car for a good price rather than use it until fit only for the scrap heap. Work-breaks have an essential part to play. Having an hour off for lunch is obviously important, especially as it gives you the chance to get out-of-doors. The best position for shorter breaks is just after the peak of morning and afternoon work — say 11.00 a.m. and 4.00 p.m. We tend to work harder, as if putting in a spurt, just before and sometimes just after a break. Anticipation plays a part here. Also the value of the work-break depends upon its length and the way in which it is spent. If the break is too long it will waste time, or it may do positive harm by loss of mental momentum — the equivalent to a sportsman's muscles hardening up. If it is too short it will interrupt you without reducing your fatigue.

Now you can see why an hour or two before breakfast is the best time for most people. You have the benefit of the natural surge of energy at dawn. There is a work-break prospect in the shape of breakfast, the best meal of the day for many of us. Above all the rest of the world seems to be still asleep, and so you have solitude and silence. There are still more benefits. Once your mental engine is running and warm it is easy to keep going fast and hard after breakfast during that key period between 9.00 a.m. and noon. Finally, it is difficult not to feel a sense of self-satisfaction that you have managed to get up early and have been productive while others have slept away the best of the day!

A possible disadvantage if you make getting up early a habit is that you will feel even more tired than usual at 3.00 p.m. and positively sleepy at dinnertime. You may be able to take a nap at lunch time. Or you may find as you grow older that you can manage on less sleep anyway. If not, there is no rule that says you must always get up each day at the same time. Flexibility of mind and a good alarm clock is all you need.

HOW TO BE MORE CREATIVE

Creative thinking cannot be forced. If you are working on a problem and getting nowhere, it is often best to leave it for a while and let your subconscious mind take over. Your mind does not work by the clock although it likes deadlines. Sometimes the answer will come to you in the middle of the night.

Grasping the principle of the 'depth mind' — as I call the subconscious and unconscious part of the brain — could open the door for you to make the best use of your best time. Many people are still not even aware that their depth minds can carry out important mental functions for them, such as synthesizing parts into new wholes or establishing new connections while they are engaged in other activities.

Imagine your mind is like a personal telex machine. It would be nice and tidy if you could sit down for an hour each morning before breakfast and receive inspired telex messages from your depth mind. But it isn't like that. The telex machine might start whirring at any time of the day or night.

The whole creative thinking process can be described thus:

PREPARATION The hard work. You have to collect and sort the relevant information, analyse the problem as thoroughly as you can, and explore possible solutions.

INCUBATION This is the depth mind phase. Mental work — analysing, synthesizing and valuing — continues on the problem in your subconscious mind. The parts of the problem separate and new combinations occur. These may involve other ingredients stored away in your memory.

INSIGHT The 'Eureka' moment. A new idea emerges into your conscious mind, either gradually or suddenly like a fish flashing out of the water. These moments often occur when you are not thinking about the problem but are in a relaxed frame of mind.

VALIDATION This is where your valuing faculty comes into play. A new idea, insight, intuition, hunch or solution needs to be thoroughly tested. This is especially so if it is to form the basis for action of any kind.

If you are using prime time for thinking along a certain line and nothing happens, stop. Instead of investing more time — throwing good money after bad — analyse the problem again and see if you can come up with a new approach. Usually your frustration will be caused by one of the following mental roadblocks.

Lack of facts	If you are not sure you have all the relevant and available facts, you naturally hesitate to commit yourself. Do some more research and that may get you moving again.
Lack of conviction	Maybe you are finding it difficult because you lack conviction in this particular project or the way in which you have been asked to do it. Re-establish a worthwhile objective.
Lack of a starting point	Possibly the task seems so large that you don't know where to start. If so, make a start anywhere. You can always change it later. Inspiration comes after you've started, not before.
Lack of perspective	Perhaps you are too close to the problem, especially if you have lived with it a long time or have been worrying about it incessantly. Try leaving it for a week. Consult others. Simply explaining it to them may help. They may see new angles.
Lack of motivation	Do you want it to happen enough? Creative thinking requires perseverance in the face of surmountable difficulty. If you are too easily put off it may be a sign that deep down you lack the necessary motivation. Re-invigorate your sense of purpose.

Fig. 7.2   *Mental Roadblocks*

The processes of analysing a problem or identifying an objective are themselves means of programming the mind. Possible solutions and courses of action almost instantly begin to occur to us. Where there is a time delay this means that the deeper parts of the brain have been summoned into action and have made what contribution they can.

Do you believe in the depth mind? By belief I don't mean that you are merely prepared to assent to the proposition that it exists, or even that it can work creatively for some people. By belief I mean something akin to personal faith. Do you *trust* your depth mind? Do you accept that it can, does and will work for you?

If your answer is an unreserved "Yes" or a more cautious "I hope so" or "I would like to think so" some consequences for action follow. The fundamental principle is to work with nature, not against it. Elsewhere, in *Effective Decision Making* (1984), I have described the natural processes of the mind at work, including the depth mind dimension. You will see there how important *preparation time* is for creative thinking: careful and clear analysis, conscious imagining or synthesizing (using such techniques as brainstorming and solo brainstorming), and exercising the valuing function of thought in a positive rather than negative way.

If you are planning to experiment and try a session before breakfast it is useful always to have a preparation phase the night before. Imagine yourself as a house decorator, scraping down the woodwork and filling in holes and priming here and there, prior to painting a first coat next day.

MOONLIGHTING

Sometimes you will find that you awaken naturally in the early hours of the morning and then lie awake with ideas tumbling over each other in your mind. Again, be flexible. Resist the idea that you must go back to sleep simply because you are in bed and beds are for sleeping. Instead, make notes about the ideas while they are fresh in your mind. (You will need to keep a notepad by your bed for this purpose.) Then you can go back to sleep. Moonlighting, this particular form of Adair's Law of the Depth Mind, has also been found, paradoxically, to be an excellent cure for insomnia. Indeed last year I was awarded a Gold Medal by the North Carolina branch of Insomniacs International, who regarded the concept of moonlighting as a significant contribution to what has become a major managerial stress disease. My wife maintains they gave it to me because my books put people to sleep!

THE PARETO PRINCIPLE

The Pareto principle, named after an Italian economist, states that the significant items of a given group form a relatively small part of the total. For example, 20 per cent of the sales force will bring in 80 per cent of new business. As that ratio seems to hold true in many areas, it is often called the 80/20 rule or the concept of 'the vital few and trivial many.'

Other writers have already applied the principle to time management. It is especially useful in coping with daily lists of action points. Most of the benefit will be related to two or three of the items. Select these key items and allocate blocks of consolidated time to achieve them.

The Pareto principle also relates to the time available in your day. Eighty per cent of your really productive and creative work will be done in 20 per cent of your time. Not just any old 20 per cent. By now you should know clearly which 4 to 5 hours of the day constitute your prime time.

KEY POINTS

● Your best time is simply when you do your best work. For most people it is early in the morning, with performance tailing off by lunchtime. Use this time for your most important work. The early bird usually catches the worm.

● You will get the most out of your prime hours if you give some study to the laws of creative thinking. Preparation in the form of problem analysis and information collecting is especially valuable. Understanding how your mind works, especially the depth mind principle, is a great help. It enables you to work with nature and not against it.

● 'Chance only favours invention for minds that are prepared for it by patient study and persevering efforts,' wrote Pasteur.

● Most of us have experienced solutions to problems that have come when we have 'slept on it'. In other words, silently but surely your depth mind has been working for you. Creative ideas often come when you are working early in the morning. Be ready for them like a fisherman waiting on a riverbank.

● Moonlighting means working in bed in the early hours of the morning. If your mental activity looks like being fruit-ful turn the light on and take some notes. One entrepreneur dreamt of a brilliant new product but forgot to write the dream down. Next day he had forgotten it and was furious with himself. Fortunately he had the same dream next night and wrote it down. Now he is a millionaire.

● Twenty per cent of your time will produce 80 per cent of your productive output. Can you afford not to manage at least *that* 20 per cent? Start tomorrow with those four or five hours and it will change your life.

> *'Mind, it is our best work that He wants,*
> *not the dregs of our exhaustion. I think He*
> *must prefer quality to quantity.'*
>
> *George MacDonald*

8. Time Effectiveness In Offices

Most of us work in offices. They range from palatial suites in the headquarters of large organisations to the single room of a professional or self-employed person.

As you progress in managing your time well you will increasingly become aware of the dangers posed by office life. For offices are inhabited by other people. They may not use their own time to good effect. Even worse, they may misuse your time or frustrate your efforts in a hundred ways.

Don't misunderstand me; I believe passionately in the value of working with others. Teamwork is an essential and enjoyable element in most jobs. But there is a vast difference between the rare phenomenon of a high-performance team and most work groups. One key characteristic of such a team is that each individual member uses both his or her own time and the time of the other members to good effect.

Just as many products now carry a public health warning so certain offices should also carry a time warning: WORKING IN THIS OFFICE COULD DAMAGE YOUR TIME.

Whether or not your office comes into this category does not simply depend upon the attitudes and skills of your colleagues or staff. Imagine for a moment that your office is a watering-hole in the African bush. Predators know where to find game at these places at certain hours. Major time-wasters equally know where you will be if they are hungry for your lifeblood of time.

The object of this chapter is to help you to transform your office into a platform for effective action. After reading it you should be clear about the principle of time management in offices and have some ideas about applying them next week to your own office.

OFFICE ARRANGEMENT

Time can be wasted imperceptibly if your work area isn't organised well. Of course you shouldn't become obsessional about office furnishings. A symptom of a status-conscious person is precisely this constant anxiety over the quality of carpet or size of desk. But you should strive to develop a well-ordered office, one that will allow you maximum freedom to pursue your work effectively.

As an individual you will naturally differ from others in your likes and dislikes over office organisation. Work habits vary. But you should test your habits against a consensus of the habits of successful executives given below. It may be that you have picked up some bad ones on the way. If so, these malfunctioning routines need modifying, if not dropping altogether.

Your office should be arranged in the light of the functions you perform. Equipment and materials which you use often need to be close to you. For example, if you use a typewriter often each day it should be within reach — not where you have to walk to find it.

Physical comfort and aesthetic satisfaction are important factors. You may have walked into your office sometimes and been depressed by the disorder: papers piled high, unwashed coffee cups, dust and dirt, unwashed windows and dreary decoration. Change it! It is surprising how much better everyone feels if the office is freshly decorated, the walls lightened and hung with some pictures or prints, well carpeted, and with some fresh flowers or green plants to be seen.

Good lighting is especially important in order to prevent tired eyes and headaches. Desk-level lighting should always be considered, for it is more concentrated than overhead lighting. It also cuts down on noise, as people tend to walk slower and talk lower in areas of localized light.

Never grudge the expense of buying comfortable and well-designed chairs for yourself and your staff. That doesn't mean you should buy one of those plush chairs like first-class airline seats. Backache is a common disease and it afflicts those who sit for long hours in badly-designed chairs. Take advice and buy chairs which enable people to work without straining their backs or inducing unnecessary physical fatigue.

The actual plan of your office should be reviewed. If you are a more senior manager or executive your office should ideally be arranged with a working area and a meeting area. Here is one possible office design:

Fig. 8.1 *Office Design*

Your desk should be placed so that you have to turn away from it in order to face and talk to a visitor. If you talk to a person over a desk it can seem a barrier — if not a barricade — between the two of you.

If you do much writing and are right-handed, the source of daylight should normally come from the left. Not having the window directly in front of you may also cut down possible distraction from outside.

An adequate work surface is essential. In this respect an office is like a kitchen. A desk is insufficient. You will also need a work table or counter adjoining your desk or immediately behind you.

If you travel extensively, somewhere to hang clothes and keep luggage can save time. If you lack a suitable annexe to your office for this purpose a small wardrobe can provide enough space.

You may notice that the conference table in Fig. 8.1 is a round one. You will recall that the legendary King Arthur had the first round table built. Unlike an oblong table it militated against tiresome quarrels over precedence among his knights. Nobody could argue that they were placed below the salt. A round table symbolizes a high degree of equality. It emphasizes the true nature of council, which is that all should speak their minds without fear or favour. "When we have a problem," writes one manager in Shell who accepted a suggestion from one of his people and bought a round table for his office, "we get together the best people to address it and we are all equals in that discussion. Often we get very good ideas from the more junior people and it is important that they feel free to participate. Somehow a round table seems both practical and appropriate."

THE ART OF DESKMANSHIP

Your desk should be clear of all paper except the specific job in hand. That invites you to think about one thing at a time. Concentration is a great time-saver.

Take an objective look at your desk the next time you sit down at it. Is there a clutter of papers, letters and files sitting on it? If left unmolested clutter creates in you a feeling of being 'snowed under' resulting in tension and frustration. As a first step, clear up your desk and files in order to cut down the amount of time needed to search for items. If in doubt ask yourself, "What's the worst thing that will happen if I throw this away?"

Once your desk is clear check that it's organised so that you don't spend time searching for things like felt-tip pens, paperclips, ruler, scissors, stapler, paper, envelopes, memo pads and so on. Remember again the wise old rule — *A place for every-thing and everything in its place.*

Think of your desk as both a work bench and tool chest. Many managers act as if their desks are four-sided wastepaper baskets, or storage depots for odds-and-ends, or flat surfaces for stacking correspondence and files. One manager, who kept a careful record of his time, discovered one week that he had spent 1 hour and 17 minutes searching for key papers on top of or in the drawers of his desk!

PAPERWORK

Having sorted through your files and weeded out the papers that can be safely thrown away, you are now ready to tackle new papers — the material which arrives in various forms on your desk each day.

The principle that is often recommended is *to handle each piece of paper only once.* It's been called the million pound idea. Managers who have discovered and applied it have saved up to one hour a day or 220 hours a year. Don't put down a letter or memo that needs a response until you have fired off a reply. It's often easier to think of an answer when you've just read a letter and your reaction is fresh in your mind.

Alternatively it has been suggested that anything worth read-ing deserves reading more than once. Certainly a decision will sometimes require more thought and you may not be able to reply at once. If so, do something to move ahead the project that the paper alludes to, even if it's only a decision to seek advice or to determine when you'll review the matter again.

Disposing of a letter or report in this decisive way requires constant practice and an iron will. But it is the key to handling paperwork and so it is worth acquiring the habit.

If paper arrives by the sackload do not panic. Sort the daily mountain into piles according to priority:

FOR ACTION	If you can take complete action, do so at once. If that is not possible, take action, e.g. mark on it what action is needed, then consign to pending tray or file. Have an effective 'brought forward' system.
FOR INFORMATION	Read and then file or throw away or pass on duly initialled. Comment directly on the paper wherever possible.
FOR READING	This is material which does not need to be read at once. Save it for marginal time.
FOR WASTE PAPER	If the paper fits into none of the above categories consign it speedily to the wastepaper basket.

Fig. 8.2   *The Paperwork Mountain*

Put the highest priority from the immediate action pile in the centre of your desk and put the remainder on a work surface. You can only think about one thing at a time. You can only focus on one task at a time. Concentrate all your attention on that item.

It is worth keeping a bottom drawer or file for paper which you deliberately want to leave alone unless someone asks for it. I call it the Procrastination Drawer. Procrastination is a time-consuming habit, but calculated or deliberate procrastination is a weapon in your armoury. Use it selectively and occasionally. Some problems if left alone will solve themselves. If someone shouts for it, you can always say you have been studying it and then get down to work rapidly. It's a bit risky, but you can save hours tackling some tasks that may evaporate before you've done your required work. Review the drawer from time to time, and never use it to put off a task you know you should do.

A final rule: clearing your desk completely, or at least leaving it in good order, should become a habit. No good workman will ever leave his workbench strewn with blunt tools, wood shavings and pots of congealed glue at the end of the day. A clear desk is a foundation for tomorrow's work.

PAPERWORK: THE MARKS & SPENCER METHOD

In 1956 Sir Simon Marks, the Chairman of Marks & Spencer, noticed two managers at one store working overtime checking stockcards. He found that a million of these cards were being filled in every year. After investigation it was found that these cards were not necessary and could be replaced by much simpler methods of inventory checking, such as spot checks, setting stockroom staff free to replenish supplies when stocks ran low.

This success led the company to launch a campaign against excessive paperwork. Every file, memo and form, every kind of paperwork was examined. Managers were asked "Would the business collapse if we dispensed with this form?"

Some 26 million pieces of paper or card, a total of 120 tons of paper, were eliminated in the first year. For example, time-sheets were thrown away and the responsibility of ensuring good timekeeping was given to supervisors.

These principles of eliminating or simplifying paperwork have continued to be rigorously applied in Marks & Spencer. The guiding policy is "If in doubt, throw it out."

The realization that people can be trusted to follow general guidelines is a cornerstone of the war on paper. Otherwise manuals of detailed instructions and written reports as the only means of control will multiply.

Another key principle is the idea of 'sensible approximation'. It means that getting figures close enough for all practical purposes makes more sense than seeking perfection. As Sir Simon Marks said, "Those who make a fetish of perfection are wasting time and money which could be better allocated elsewhere."

HOW TO WRITE AND READ EFFECTIVELY

While on the subject of paperwork it is worth reviewing your basic skills of writing and reading. Advanced proficiency in them is a sure way to conserve your time.

Let's start with writing skills. For you are a generator of paperwork through your pen or typewriter as well as a consumer. In the nightmare war of paperwork are you part of the solution or are you part of the problem?

Clarity, simplicity and conciseness are the essentials of business writing. If you can add to them strength, vigour and tone you will produce high-quality papers or letters. You will also be able to write more of them in less time.

How do you develop the habit of clear, simple and concise writing? One method is to discipline yourself to follow a systematic approach, whether you are dictating a letter or writing a paper. Aim first for an orderly outline:

THINK	What is my purpose in writing? Pinpoint the message. Find the heart of the letter you are answering. Underline the key issue or question that should be answered. Try to visualize the reader.
LIST	Jot down each thought that you want to express on a scrap of paper
ARRANGE	Put your points in a logical order, discarding the irrelevant ones

Fig. 8.3   *Steps to Clarity of Expression*

Do not cover too many subjects in one letter, as you run the risk of overloading the reader with information. Remember

that the reader will tend to fasten attention on the most interesting point and disregard your other pearls.

Keep it short and simple. Shortness is achieved by not over-
burdening the reader with too much data. Edit out any irrelevant, overlong or repetitive sentences. Strive to write one-page
letters or memos — they are more digestible. For your reader's
sake avoid jargon, ambiguity and formal language. Write con-
versationally, using short sentences and familiar words.

Reading skills once acquired can save time. Speed-reading
courses are not the answer. Few people who complete speed-
reading courses maintain the speeds reached under training. It
is better to save time by cutting out all reading that is only of
marginal value than to learn to gallop through everything by
speed-reading methods.

Now that the photocopier has added immeasurably to the
paper which is produced and distributed in organisations it is
essential to develop your ability to scan through, say, a report
quickly and accurately. Do not assume that you must read
every word. Treat it like a newspaper. Start with the headlines
on the cover. Then look at the introduction, where the author
tells you his aims and the method he has adopted. Then glance
at the table of contents. Try to identify the key ideas in each
chapter or section. Read details only when they are related to a
key idea important to you. Using this method, you can become
proficient at gutting a report or book in a remarkably short
time.

Don't always read at top gear. Occasionally you may come
across a passage, paper or book that will be profoundly useful
to you in the future. Don't rush through it now. Read it once
or twice at your leisure, making notes on it. By this method its
message will become a part of you.

MAKE THE TELEPHONE WORK FOR YOU

The telephone is a great time-saving tool — in the right hands.
By using it you can obtain information that would take you
days or weeks by letter. Not only does it save time but a telephone conversation can cut down the considerable expenses of
travel. Unlike a letter it gives you the opportunity for spoken
dialogue with the other person. It is usually inferior in value to

an actual meeting, but it is often better than correspondence.

How much time do you spend on the telephone? Some research suggests that managers can over-estimate or underestimate the time taken up in this way by as much as 50 per
cent. If you haven't done so already try keeping a time log
specifically on your telephone time — both incoming and out-
going calls — for one week. Use a stopwatch to give some
precision to your self-study.

On completion your first reaction may be "I didn't know I
talked that long." Here are some rules-of-thumb for making
better use of the telephone.

● *Planning* Make a habit of planning each telephone call you
make, using an abbreviated form of the system
suggested above for letters. Make a brief note of
what you want to say or what you wish to find
out, so that the object of the call is clear in your
mind. This will save both your time and the time
of the person on the other end of the telephone.
Your aim is concise, clear and friendly communication.

● *Batching* Set aside a period of time each day for making
and — if possible — receiving telephone calls. By
bunching your calls before lunch or towards the
end of the day, when people are less inclined
towards verbosity, you can get through your telephoning much more economically.

● *Timing* Buy an egg-timer — the sandglass variety — and
place it by the telephone. Aim to complete suc-
cessfully every telephone conversation in three
minutes without introducing a sense of haste or,
worse still, a tone of brusqueness. Keep a score
and see if you can reduce your failure rate each
week.

Telephone control makes practical good sense. A pro-
ductivity rise of no less than 23 per cent in one year has been
reported by the Northwestern Mutual Life Insurance
Company after the introduction of a quiet hour, one day a

week, when incoming telephone calls are shut off to let work continue uninterrupted.

HOW TO CONTROL INTERRUPTIONS

"Time is a dressmaker specializing in alterations," said the writer Faith Baldwin. Much of your time will be taken up with unplanned alterations. Your carefully planned day can often end in shreds.

To repeat a point made earlier, don't assume that all interventions are interruptions of your time. You must look at so-called interruptions in perspective. What appears to be an interruption may well be a matter of high priority to the person interrupting. When you have listened it may prove to be so for you too. In other words, there are good interruptions and bad ones. An act of judgement precedes your response. It filters interruptions, determining how much time if any you can give to each.

You can't eliminate interruptions. Many of them, as we have seen, are requests that you do whatever job you are being paid to do. Remember that doctor mentioned earlier. It would be inappropriate for him or her to refuse to be interrupted when on call. Talking to patients, answering an anxious mother's question, responding to an emergency call — these are what the doctor's job is all about.

Still, you should plan in order to minimize the number of unwelcome interruptions if you're going to manage effectively. One hour of concentrated work is worth four hours broken into five-minute fragments by unwanted callers or trivial telephone queries. To re-immerse yourself in a report after each interruption takes time. So the real time cost of an interruption is much more than the actual time your visitor spends in your office.

Learning to manage these negative interruptions takes resolve and practice. Here are some guidelines for keeping interruptions as short as possible:

● Set a time limit and stick to it. Say "I have five minutes — will that do or would you rather fix a time later?"

● Set the stage in advance: you are very busy with a deadline in sight.

● With casual droppers-in remain standing. If they sit down, perch on the edge of your desk.

● Meet in the other person's office — you can then determine when to leave.

● Avoid small talk when you are busy; it doubles interruption time.

● Get them to the point. Don't be afraid to interrupt the interrupter, asking him what is the problem? What is the purpose of his call?

● Be ruthless with time but gracious with people. Give them your full attention. Listen well. Be firm but friendly and helpful. Do not let them go away empty-handed if you can avoid it.

● Have a clock available where visitors can see it, and don't be afraid to glance at it a few times. Explain about your next appointment; a white lie is better than a black interruption.

● Use a call-back system for telephone calls, unless they are important enough to be put through at once.

The person who interrupts you most in your office is — no, not your boss, he or she comes second — it is you yourself. Sometimes we are all itching to be interrupted. Usually when you are tackling a chore or about to undertake an unpleasant task it is a delight to be interrupted. You wait for the telephone to ring. Or you suddenly take it into your head to call up a colleague about a totally unimportant matter, thereby interrupting someone else. "No, No, nothing urgent — just ringing for a chat."

You can also interrupt yourself in a variety of ways: making coffee, dropping one project and starting another, gossiping with your secretary or a colleague you hi-jacked in the corridor, or keeping people too long at meetings. Despite protestations to the contrary you are 'asking for it.' You *need* interruptions. Beware of yourself, interruption master in disguise.

YOUR PROFESSIONAL ASSISTANT

Office secretary, personal assistant, Girl Friday: many are the names given to your professional assistant. By whatever name they are known they are vital to your success. His or her title should reflect the specific contribution which that person makes to the organisation.

There are different kinds of secretaries, corresponding to different levels of professional knowledge and skill, just as managers vary in their kinds and degrees of competence. As a general rule senior managers should have higher-grade secretaries. They are best regarded as *professional assistants* — not personal assistants — even though they may contrive to be known as secretaries. Old names die hard.

If your secretary has become part of your effective working team, then you have indeed a professional assistant, one who is a real asset both to you and the organisation. He or she should be highly trained in all aspects of office management — communications and human relations as well as individual skills of shorthand, typing, filing and telephone technique. In other words, he or she is a real professional and one of your chief time-savers in the office.

The secretaries of some of today's chief executives already have a personal computer, one or two printers, a word processor, an electronic typewriter and a closed-circuit TV. Such secretaries spend less time serving coffee or typing and more time on administration, information collection and retrieval, and data interpretation, analysis and collection.

Simultaneously and somewhat ironically, personal computers and electronic mail can make it easier for a manager to type and send his own messages. Instead of reviewing their secretaries' work, some managers now find that their secretaries are checking their efforts at computing in its various forms.

Office automation can free your secretary to perform essential administrative functions. These include helping you to save time by:

● Keeping unwanted callers at bay, on the telephone or in person. They may think they must see you, but if your PA is fully briefed he or she may be able to divert them to the appropriate person.

● Minimizing interruptions. Your PA can arrange interviews at times you have reserved for that purpose in your diary or arrange for you to telephone them at times convenient to you.

● Dealing with routine correspondence herself. Forms can be filled in or applications for such things as parking permits can be dealt with instead of landing on your desk.

Your professional assistant can only help you to manage your time better if you respect his or her time. That means refraining from needless interrupting. Try to bunch your requests, so that your PA has time to get on with jobs. Avoid chopping and changing your mind about priorities once you've told him or her what to do.

Use a pocket dictaphone to deal with correspondence unless you need your secretary's input to the letter in question. You can dictate letters by the batch when it suits you, on a train journey for example, and your secretary can type them when it suits him or her.

Don't be a perfectionist. The less you fuss over details the better. Excellence is not the same as perfection. A good office team will strive for excellence but eschew the expensive and illusory goal of perfection. Nothing frustrates a secretary more than a perfectionist manager, who must dot every i and cross every t himself. When you are next tempted to order a whole report to be retyped because you have spotted some minor error of grammar or spelling, remember that the Declaration of Independence has the odd slip or mistake in it, yet it has communicated remarkably well.

In short, your secretary is an integral part of a work team. Treat him or her as a professional, not as a servant.

KEY POINTS

● Take a close look at your office when you next go into it. Have you organised it, or does it organise you?

● A desk is a work bench for paperwork. Check that it is cleared for action at the end of each day. The essential tools of your trade should be readily at hand, so that you don't waste time searching for things.

● Work out a system for sorting incoming paper. See if you can apply the principle of handling each piece of paper only once.

● Like driving a car, writing and reading can be done with skill. Clear, simple and concise writing saves your time and the time of your readers. With practice you can also learn to read faster: by swiftly and accurately recognising what not to read or what can be scanned rather than absorbed.

● Telephones are potentially great time-savers. In the wrong hands they can fragment your day.

● Distinguish between interruptions. Some are good; some are tolerable; and some are avoidable. A conscious act of judgement should govern your response. Once you are interrupted employ some of the damage-control hints given in this chapter.

● The mirror will always reveal to you the number one interrupter in your life.

● If you have a secretary transform him or her into a professional assistant. Such a person has a strategic importance in your battle to use your time on the right things in office hours.

> *'Time wastes our bodies and our wits,*
> *But we waste Time, so we are quits.'*

>   *Sundial, 1746*

9. Managing Meetings

"Meetings, bloody meetings" sums up what you may think about meetings. Do the meetings you attend seem like a necessary evil, distracting you from your main business?

Attending too many badly organised meetings certainly engenders that attitude. If the basis for getting together is dubious in the first place, if the discussion drags on and the conclusions are unclear, it is not surprising that the overall experience is negative. "What a waste of valuable time," you mutter to yourself as the doors finally open.

What is a meeting? Here the word means a preplanned arrangement for people to come together at a given time and place to do something, such as exchange information or make a decision. Meetings are distinguished here from interviews, which are basically on a one-to-one basis. The key principles of meetings set out below do apply to interviews as well, but other factors — such as question-asking technique — also have to be taken into account. Although unplanned or informal meetings and interviews do take up a great deal of your time this chapter will only focus upon programmed meetings of more than two people.

There are, of course, many positive aspects to meetings. You cannot run any work group, team or organisation without them. They are necessary, even essential, and often enjoyable — for we are social beings who delight in conversational give-and-take with each other. But meetings are still potential time-wasters. Other people may be more in control of the meeting than you are, and they may be cavalier with your time. Even if you are in the chair you may find pressures upon you to extend the meeting unduly or even to hijack it for purposes other than the stated objectives.

The remedy for these potential time hazards lies in developing your skills both as leader (chairman) and as a team member. Do your meetings always, as a matter of policy, begin on time and end on time? Acquire the ability to budget accurately the time requirement in advance. Remember Parkinson's Law. Always negotiate time limits with other participants when they arrive before getting down to business: it will focus everyone's minds and energies to work against an agreed deadline.

DIFFERENT KINDS OF MEETINGS

In order to practise and perfect these time management skills it is useful to recognise the main categories of meetings in working life. Each has its particular nature and challenges. In real life any given meeting may have elements of two or three of the following types, but you will save time and conserve effort if you are able to make clear when you are changing gear from one to the other.

A BRIEFING MEETING

A briefing meeting is called by the manager to direct or instruct his subordinates to undertake a particular task or to lay down policy governing future conduct. It is characterized by:

    giving instructions and information

    clearing up misunderstandings

    integrating ideas and views where appropriate

AN ADVISORY MEETING

An advisory meeting is called essentially for the exchange of information. It is not a decision-making meeting as such. It is characterized by:

    seeking advice about a problem

    informing others about ideas

    listening to views

A COUNCIL MEETING

A council meeting is held between people of equal standing who have some professional knowledge or skill to contribute to the matter in hand. It is characterized by:

decisions being made by consensus

accountability lying with the group

resolving differences by 'talking through' them

A COMMITTEE MEETING

A committee meeting is one in which representatives from various groups or interests meet on a roughly equal footing to make decisions on matters of common concern. It is characterized by:

a sense of authority

differences ultimately being resolved by voting

compromises being common

A NEGOTIATING MEETING

A negotiating meeting is also one in which representatives of different interests meet, but decisions are made more on a bargaining basis than by voting. It is characterized by:

decisions being taken on a *quid pro quo* basis

each side having different but overlapping aims

each side seeking to achieve best terms for itself

Fig. 9.1   *Five Types of Meetings*

Council or collegiate meetings are worth special mention because they are becoming more important as the professional knowledge and skill available in companies increases. Decisions in such meetings are usually made by consensus. That does not mean the decision in question is a given member's preferred solution. But it does mean he or she will accept it as the optimum decision in the situation and *be prepared to act upon it.* If members fail to implement a decision without cause it is a sure sign that the meeting reached a false consensus.

If a person disagrees at any point, he has to make clear his reason and contribute towards an alternative course of action that would be generally acceptable. For example, in a meeting on the construction of a new building there needs to be a consensus between the accountants, architects and builders. If the accountants told the architects that the proposed building was too expensive in terms of the company's funds, then a joint reappraisal would have to be done. It would be senseless for the architects and builders to ignore the accountants. It would be equally inappropriate for the accountants to turn a deaf ear to what the builders had to say about safety standards. They have to work it through until a consensus is reached on what is the optimum building which will yield an acceptable profit, meet the needs of the customer, look good and be completely safe.

The distinctive feature of the work of a council-type of meeting is that several minds in co-operation, on the basis of a substantial degree of equality, are needed to make the decision. The decision is therefore the decision of the group as a whole and each member is bound by it. He accepts it even though he disagrees. If the matter does not permit of compromise, it is his duty to resign. For this reason in a well conducted council meeting it should seldom be found necessary to take a vote. If the chairman cannot sum up the sense of the meeting in a form which the members will accept, the matter is probably not yet ripe for decision by that body. This is, in fact, what happens at meetings of most boards of directors; only very occasionally is a vote taken.

The way people sit at tables and the shape of the table itself can tell much about the purpose of the meeting. The round table aptly symbolizes and best serves the council type of meeting. It emphasizes the lack of a pecking order: all seats around it but one (that of the leader) are of equal importance. In Chapter Seven, I have suggested the round table should become more of a feature in managers' offices. Some innovative individual managers and companies are already disposing of their square tables — symbols of hierarchical models of management — and are introducing round tables into their offices. For a round table encourages a team approach to decision-making and problem-solving, with the leader leading by competence — not because he sits at the head of the table.

It is important that meetings should be used for the purpose for which they are best suited. Two matters on which a committee decision may well be more valuable than an individual's decision are:—

(i) questions of general policy or major decisions where the interplay of various interests and factors needs to be balanced; these tend to be matters which do not require immediate decisions and when a period of gestation may be valuable, though there are plenty of examples of committees which take decisions more quickly than could be done by individual consultation;

(ii) matters which for various reasons need to be de-personalised; for example, where personal predilection and bias need to run the gauntlet of criticism by others and to be recognised as having done so.

THE COST OF MEETING

Managers spend much time in meetings of all kinds and consequently meetings are expensive. It is important to develop a sense of the financial cost of meetings as a step towards the better management both of your time and of the time of other people. The following chart gives you a picture of the cost of a person's time in ratio to their salaries.

The following figures are based on a working year of 238 days with one working day equal to seven hours. Overheads are not included. The chart highlights how costly time wasting can be at various salary levels.

Salary/Annum £	5 mins	15 mins	1 hour	1 day
35,000	£1.75	£5.25	£21.00	£147.00
30,000	£1.50	£4.50	£18.00	£126.00
25,000	£1.25	£3.75	£15.00	£105.00
20,000	£1.00	£3.00	£12.00	£84.00
15,000	£0.75	£2.25	£ 9.00	£63.00

Fig. 9.2   *The Cost of Your Time*

The obvious question to ask yourself before every meeting is:

IS THIS MEETING REALLY NECESSARY?

All too often people meet for the sake of meeting. Getting together at a regular time becomes a habit. It is possible that the original purpose for that particular group of people to come together has been fulfilled. Or the purpose may need re-definition. If so, you should review who should be involved, as well as the place and time of the meeting.

Before you call your next meeting consider the other options, not least because they are more economical in money as well as time. Could the matter be dealt with by letter, memorandum, telephone calls or meetings with individuals? Sometimes ten minutes spent with six people individually is more productive than trying to get them all together for an hour.

Check on the composition of the meeting. Make sure the meeting isn't larger than it needs to be. Do all managers need to attend all meetings? Be wary of arguments like "They've always come along" or "We can't risk offending him by not inviting him," or "You never can tell, we might just need him." The presence of too many people cuts down the time every individual has to contribute to the discussion.

It is a good idea to review all the meetings you attend — especially on a regular basis — at least twice a year.

The Regular Meetings Analysis Sheet (Fig. 9.3) is designed to help you to do this review. As a result of completing the sheet with a particular committee meeting to view you may decide, for example, that you can safely switch from regular to occasional attendance, or from being there for the whole meeting to attending only for those items on the agenda which concern you or your department. Information about the other business can usually be gleaned from the minutes — if they are properly kept and circulated — in a way which is much more time-efficient for you.

With meetings in mind may I remind you of the importance of learning to say no (see p. 62). People often accumulate regular meetings commitments because they cannot bring themselves to say no in the first place or to extricate themselves from meetings they have unwisely agreed to attend. Over-commitment soon leads to ineffectiveness.

MEETING:

PURPOSE (in one sentence):

MEMBERS:

FREQUENCY:

AVERAGE DURATION:

RANK IMPORTANCE (on a scale of O—Useless to
10—Absolutely Essential):
  (1) To me:
  (2) To organisation:

COMMENTS:

SHOULD I ATTEND: Full time   Action required:
                   Part time
                   Occasionally
                   Not at all

DATE FOR NEXT REVIEW:

Fig. 9.3   *Regular Meetings Analysis Sheet*

PREPARING FOR AN EFFECTIVE MEETING

Careful preparation is the secret of time-effective meetings.
First and foremost, is is essential that the chairman be clear
about the objective or objectives of the proposed meeting. It
may by one of any of the five types identified in Fig. 9.1, or a
combination of them. Within those categories the actual purpose needs to be crystal clear. A useful way of double-checking

is to ask yourself "Where should we all be at the end of this meeting?"

The agenda is a key factor. It shouldn't be just a list of headings to jog your memory during a meeting. Draw it up with thought, indicating whether an item is for discussion or decision. Briefly describe the matter or subject. 'Mounting costs', for example, looks too brief and vague, whereas 'Mounting costs: to discuss the report on energy conservation in the factory and make decisions on the first and third recommendations on p.16' is much more definite. It gives people the opportunity to think about the matter beforehand. Ensure that everyone receives the agenda and relevant papers — in this case the energy conservation report — at least five clear days before the meeting.

People take in information more readily through their eyes than their ears. Hence the Chinese proverb, 'A picture is worth a thousands words', Therefore visual aids should more often than not play a part in your meetings: if they are clear, simple and vivid they can save you time.

Exercise Be Prepared

Identify the next three formal meetings which you will chair. Jot them down on a piece of paper and label them A, B and C. Do you intend to make use of any of the following:

	A	B	C
— Overhead projector	...	...	...
— Slides	...	...	...
— Prepared flipcharts	...	...	...
— Unprepared flipcharting	...	...	...
— Reports	...	...	...
— Financial statements	...	...	...
— A written agenda	...	...	...
— Models	...	...	...
— Minutes	...	...	...
— A different room layout	...	...	...

The key preliminary steps can be summarized in the following way:

DETERMINE PURPOSE OF MEETING
Consider possible aims, such as:
To engage in joint consultation
To develop support for action
To resolve unsolved problems

EXPLORE THE SUBJECT
Collect facts and information
Identify main topics to be discussed
Consider probable differences in viewpoint

OUTLINE THE DISCUSSION
Set final objective
Consider intermediate objectives
Frame questions to develop discussion
Plan introduction specially, include main topics for discussion
Prepare timetable for meeting

HAVE EVERYTHING READY
Issue invitations and information in good time
Arrange accommodation
Prepare necessary materials, include aids such as flipcharts

Fig. 9.4   *Preparing for Meetings*

Time spent on preparation is seldom wasted. If you go into a meeting clear about the objectives, having thought about the subject in advance and with everything ready, it is already most probable that your time will be well spent.

TIMETABLING THE MEETING

The agenda is so important as a time-conserving instrument that it merits special attention here. If you are the chairman it constitutes your plan for the meeting.

Minutes of the previous meeting should usually be circulated in advance and not read through at the meeting itself.

Checking the minutes should not take long. If any substantial matters arise from them they should be noted and dealt with later in the meeting according to their level of urgency and importance.

Much time will also have been saved, as already noted, if you have circulated papers or data in advance. If this has not been possible, table it at the meeting. Having circulated a paper, however, don't read it through line by line — assume others have done their homework.

The order of items on the agenda is important, especially if the outcome of discussing one item will influence the decision on another.

Non-controversial subjects may be grouped at the beginning and the end of the meeting, so that it begins and ends on a high note. You must ensure that important subjects are discussed at a time when minds are fresh, and that argues for them being placed towards the head of the agenda.

To reiterate the first point in this chapter — the most important of all in this context — always try to fix finishing times for meetings. If you are the chairman say at the outset, "Do you think we can get this meeting over by such-and-such a time?" If you are not in the chair ask, "Have you any idea what time this meeting will end?" Everyone will have the target finishing time in their minds and you will find that this concentrates their minds and prevents long-windedness. Otherwise the principle that work expands to fill the time available for it will insinuate itself into your meeting.

Within that overall time framework, which more often than not should be agreed before people assemble and should appear on the agenda, it is good practice to allocate a time to each item and make sure that it is not grossly exceeded. Some flexibility is essential, and so you should always build into your time plan a contingency reserve of minutes which can be drawn upon at your discretion.

THE CHAIRMAN'S ROLE

Good chairmanship is vital for time-saving meetings. The chairman's task will sometimes pose problems, but a good chairman can make sure that a meeting is punctual, covers the agenda properly and achieves its objects. He or she uses your time economically and effectively.

As a chairman yourself it is useful to bear in mind that you have two principal functions within your role. Being chairman in the narrow sense means you are accountable for seeing that procedures are adhered to and that participants both behave themselves and contribute as effectively as possible to the business in hand. You are there to see fair-play, to ensure that everyone has their turn, and to apply the appropriate rules, not unlike a referee. The foreman of a jury is a chairman in this specific sense.

Secondly, you may be the group's leader or manager as well, charged with achieving specified results. The nature of those outcomes will necessarily vary according to the type of meeting (see Fig. 9.1). In creative thinking meetings, for example, the leader's role may be more that of a catalyst than traffic controller.

There can be some obvious tensions between the 'referee' and 'leader' roles. Some groups and leaders indeed seek to avoid them by appointing a referee-type chairman, like the Speaker in the House of Commons, leaving leaders free to argue their case in the meeting without having to preside over it. Other chairmen signal when they are changing hats by 'stepping down from the chair' for a particular item on the agenda.

In most situations it makes sense for the chairman to exercise both functions. There is some overlap between the two roles anyway. Let us assume here that you are doing both.

Some of the key leadership functions, such as *defining the task* and *planning,* have been discussed above. But as chairman you should remember to begin the meeting by saying what the purpose is and why it is necessary. Don't assume that everyone knows. You may also want to check that the participants are comfortable with the agenda, so that *your* plan for the meeting now becomes *our* plan for it. In a pleasant but firm way, show that you have taken charge.

Once work has started on the agenda you will have to exercise the function of *controlling,* which should be done with intelligence and sensitivity. What would you do about an over-talkative person? It is essential to stop him but it has to be done tactfully as well as firmly: "Thank you, Michael, I think we have got the drift of your argument. Susan, you haven't said anything yet. Do you agree with Michael or not?" If a long-winded person still challenges you for the right of way — by continuing to talk over others or by interrupting again — then you will have to show more steel until the message is taken. Never lose control.

CONTROLLING THE CABINET

The Cabinet usually meets once a week. That should be enough for regular meetings, and should be if they grasp from the start what they are there for. They should be back at their work as soon as possible, and a Prime Minister should put as little as possible in their way. We started sharp at 11, and rose in time for lunch. Even in a crisis, another couple of meetings should be enough in the same week: if there is a crisis, the less talk the better.

The Prime Minister shouldn't speak too much himself in Cabinet. He should start the show or ask somebody else to do so, and then intervene only to bring out the more modest chaps who, despite their seniority, might say nothing if not asked. And the Prime Minister must sum up. Experienced Labour leaders should be pretty good at this; they have spent years attending debates at meetings of the Parliamentary Party and the National Executive, and have to sum *those* up. That takes some doing — good training for the Cabinet.

Particularly when a non-Cabinet Minister is asked to attend, especially if it is his first time, the Prime Minister may have to be cruel. The visitor may want to show how good he is, and go on too long. A good thing is to take no chance and ask him to send the Cabinet a paper in advance. The Prime Minister can then say, "A very clear statement, Minister. Do you need to add anything?" in a firm tone of voice obviously expecting the answer, "*No*". If somebody else looks like making a speech, it is sound to nip in with "Has anybody any objection?" If somebody starts to ramble, a quick, "*Are you objecting?* You're not? Right. Next business," and the Cabinet can move on.

Clement Attlee

Heading off potential or actual irrelevancies is also a vital part of controlling a meeting. Sometimes a red herring looks more tasty than the bread-and-butter items on the agenda. Where the object of a meeting is creative thinking, it is often worth pursuing apparent red herrings. For the apparently irrelevant may disguise a new idea, just as an oyster shell is the unlikely bed of a pearl.

To exercise these leadership functions and to contribute yourself to the discussion, you will need to develop yourself by becoming:

● A clear and rapid thinker

● An attentive listener

● Able to express yourself clearly and succinctly

● Ready to clarify views badly expressed

● Able to be impartial and impersonal

● A preventer of inappropriate interruptions

● Patient, tolerant and kind

● Friendly but brisk and business-like

At the end of each item on the agenda the chairman should give a brief, clear and concise *summary* of what has been decided. He may even dictate the key sentence or phrase to be used in the minutes.

If someone is asked to take action as a result of discussion on an item, the chairman should check that the participant understands and accepts that action. Steps or actions thus agreed should normally carry a completion time.

The question — sometimes asked — as to whether a committee can be executive — i.e. can do anything on its own — is really trivial. Literally as a body it can no more do anything than a football team can score a goal. In each case there must be an individual agent, but it is the group which makes it possible for the individual to act. Although its decision will in most cases be carried out by one of its members, or its officers, in a real sense the action is the action of the committee. The important decision has been made by the committee, or is a consequence of its deliberations.

To ensure that action results from the work of a committee and to preserve personal responsibility, one method is to appoint as chairman of the committee not the most senior member but the member whose personal job responsibility is most in line with the responsibility of the committee.

THE ART OF MINUTING

As a guideline you as chairman should not take the minutes. That job should be delegated, possibly to your secretary. If she cannot do them then another group member should do them. If you attempt to do so it will distract you from running the meeting smoothly.

Minutes do not have to be lengthy or complicated but they should cover the following key points:

● time, date and place of meeting

● names of those present and any apologies for absence

● all items discussed, together with conclusions reached, decisions made and actions agreed

● names of those responsible for actions

● in some cases the main arguments or steps leading to decisions

● the time the meeting ended

● the date and time of the next meeting, and where it will be held

Minutes should be sent out within two or three days, especially if there are some actions to be taken fairly soon after the meeting. If full minutes are needed yet cannot be produced that soon, then a summary of actions to be taken should be listed, photocopied and sent out at once. As chairman you should sign them before they are distributed.

START ON TIME

AIM   OUTLINE PURPOSE CLEARLY˙
State problem/situation/reason
Define constraints and limitations
Establish task(s) of meeting

GUIDE   ENSURE EFFECTIVE DISCUSSION
Introduce topic(s) for discussion
Draw out opinions, viewpoints and
experiences
Develop group interest and involvement
Keep discussion within stated task(s)

CRYSTALLIZE   ESTABLISH CONCLUSIONS
Recognise degrees of feeling and
changes of opinion
Summarize points of agreement and
disagreement
State intermediate conclusions as they
are reached
Check understanding and acceptance

ACT   GAIN ACCEPTANCE AND
COMMITMENT
Summarize and state conclusion(s)
clearly
Gain commitment to action plan
State responsibility for action
Make sure that everybody understands

END ON TIME

Fig. 9.5   *Making Meetings Effective*

A SELF-DEVELOPMENT EXERCISE

You should conclude this chapter with a review of your own performance at meetings. The following exercise will help you to pinpoint the area for improvement. Transfer the headings below to a piece of blank paper, leaving space for your answers.

Exercise
In the role of chairman of meetings my strengths are:–
(Only write down strengths that are corroborated by comments or feedback you have received from others, so that you are speaking from data.)

The five areas in which I must improve are:–
(List here no more than five definite steps you can take to overcome your present weaknesses as a chairman.)

To improve the work of our meetings my group should:
(Groups, like individuals, pick up bad habits. If you were planning to run a training session for your group, what are the five lessons you would like to bring out?)

Obviously you can add other questions to this self-assessment and self-development exercise. For example, you may want to scrutinize your strengths and weaknesses as a committee member with a particular committee in mind. Surprise your colleagues by showing some enhanced skills at the next meeting. As always, build into your programme a self-review date. Never worry if your progress has not been as fast as you would like. Effort is always rewarded.

KEY POINTS

● Meetings are an inescapable part of corporate or social enterprise. Resolve to run them in a time-effective way. Begin by distinguishing between the five different kinds or purposes of meeting.

● Becoming more cost-conscious about meetings will help

you to be economical with time. Check if any given meeting is really necessary and ensure that people unnecessary for it don't have their time wasted by being required to come.

● Time spent on planning the meeting will repay itself tenfold. Work out the agenda carefully, allotting time for each item.

● As chairman you may be both referee and leader. Learn to distinguish between these two roles and blend them to perfection.

● Clear, concise and definite minutes are necessary. Although not always essential they should normally make reference to who is to do what, by when, and by when they should report back.

● Only you can improve your skills as a chairman or as an ordinary member of the group. Collect some feedback on your present performance, asking people to give some examples of your strengths and weaknesses to illustrate their general points. Then draw up an action plan to improve yourself over the next six months. Target some forthcoming meetings for practice purposes.

> *'It is essential for the Cabinet to move on, leaving in its wake a trail of clear, crisp, uncompromising decisions. That is what government is about. And the challenge to democracy is to get it done quickly.'*
>
> *Clement Attlee*

10. The Art of Delegation

Delegation has a strategic importance in the art of time management. Can you delegate effectively to others? Can you handle delegation when you are at the receiving end?

The importance of being able to delegate increases the higher up an organisation you go. In a recent survey of 280 chief executives only 30 said that they could allocate time to correspond with the relative importance of the matters facing them. You can be sure that the other 250 were not good delegators.

What is delegation? It's vital to be clear about that. For many people still confuse delegation with abdication. To relinquish totally your power to someone else is not delegation. It is an evasion of responsibility.

True delegation is not like that. It means entrusting to another person a job together with the authority to do it. Thus the delegate now acts as your agent, like the emissary of a king. If you happen to be the delegate then a task or function is committed to you by someone in authority together with the necessary powers to carry it out.

DIFFICULTIES OF DELEGATION

Delegation as a necessary principle in organisations sounds simple, and so it is. What matters in organisations is doing such simple things well, but of course in organisations it is very difficult to do simple things well. Delegation is a prime example. Nothing in organisational life is more fraught with difficulties. It either doesn't happen enough or it doesn't happen well. Both sins of omission and commission consume rather than save time. That is regrettable. For good delegation yields a double crop to the acre: it allows you to conserve time for the key functions of your job and it also develops the abilities of your subordinates.

The trouble usually starts in the realm of attitudes and values, as the following comments made to me by managers at a recent international seminar on time management illustrate:

"Personally I believe that information is power. I prefer to keep the really important details secret from my staff. If I hand that over one of them might soon be able to displace me. When I was away sick for four weeks with my ulcers the whole place almost ground to a halt, so you can see that I am indispensable to this firm now." (A senior executive in an engineering firm.)

"I favour delegation in principle, but you should see the clowns that I have working for me. They are called managers but they are not up to handling novel situations which constant technological progress and rapid market changes are creating for us now. They aren't even properly trained. Most of them have psychologically retired even if they are not yet drawing their pensions. Now you know why I carry two bulging briefcases! I just don't know what to do about it. My boss, the managing director, keeps hinting it's my fault, but I don't know what he expects me to do about it. He never tells me anyway what he expects of me." (Senior manager in a medium-sized and family-owned mechanical engineering company.)

These are symptoms partly of genuine difficulties — those inherent in the process of delegation — and partly of lack of intelligence and skill in both delegator and delegate.

Research in five European countries has unearthed the seven top reasons why chief executive officers don't delegate. Can you add any other reasons (or excuses) to the list?

1. It's risky
2. We enjoy doing things
3. We daren't sit and think
4. It's a slow process
5. We like to be 'on top of everything'
6. Will our subordinates outstrip us?
7. "Nobody can do it as well as I can"

Fig. 10.1 *Why it is difficult to delegate*

WHAT CANNOT BE DELEGATED

A visitor to the Oval office noticed a hand-lettered sign on President Truman's desk —

THE BUCK STOPS HERE

Those four words summarize an essential truth. You can delegate authority to do a job and hold that person accountable to yourself for their performance. If you do it in the right spirit and in an intelligent way you will generate a sense of responsibility in the delegate. Responsibility can be shared. But you remain *ultimately* accountable for what happens — or does not happen — in your organisation. If that burden is too heavy, re-member President Truman's other saying: "If you can't stand the heat, stay out of the kitchen."

An important corollary of that principle is that at all times sufficient control of subordinates should be maintained in order to protect your ultimate accountability.

A manager is a leader in the business settings of industry and commerce. Leadership, the core of the manager's job, is the second responsibility which cannot be delegated. That involves becoming the kind of person and acquiring the necessary skills for achieving the common task, building a team, and developing individuals. These three areas obviously overlap: in most cases, for example, you will not achieve the task unless you build teamwork among your subordinates and colleagues.

The three areas of task, team and individual, together with the key leadership functions of defining the aims and objectives, planning, controlling, evaluating, team-building and developing individuals, are general in nature. They apply to *all* leaders in *all* walks of life. Of course leaders will have to share responsibility for their effective performance with others: there is too much required for any one person to do them all. But any leader worthy of the name will not delegate his key leadership responsibilities and functions to someone else. Otherwise he will be left with an empty title and a set of status symbols while the substance of his job has fled elsewhere.

Exercise Chief Executive
You are the chief executive of a large industrial organisation in the electrical goods and electronics field, with a board of directors headed by a non-executive chairman over you. List the core responsibilities of your job: the ones that you feel that you must reserve to yourself although others, of course, will be called upon to help you to discharge them effectively. (Turn to p153 for a suggested answer after completing your list.)

Any delineation of responsibilities not withstanding, the essential responsibility of the chief executive — the main purpose of the role — is to provide leadership. Leaders should give a sense of direction: they must guide the organisation in the way. It has to be the right way, otherwise they are misleaders rather than good leaders. Leaders should inspire, especially when difficulties and obstacles abound; they should energize and build enthusiasm into the organisation.

Many parts of your job as a manager-leader can and should be delegated. But you cannot divest yourself of accountability and leadership. Lastly, you should never allow anyone else to take the decision on your behalf as to what you should delegate. That is your responsibility.

WHAT CAN BE DELEGATED

There is no set list of tasks that can be delegated. That depends upon several factors. What you can delegate in one case may not be possible to delegate in another.

It is a mistake to imagine that you either delegate or you do not. It is not as black-and-white as that. There is a continuum of delegation, depending upon the degree of control you wish to exercise. Some key points on it can be identified as follows:

| "Get on with the job; let me know what happened afterwards." | "Get on with the job, but let me know if you need advice, help or support." | "Get on with the job, but keep me closely informed of progress." | "Don't take any action on this particular point until you have consulted me." |

Fig. 10.2   *Delegation continuum*

In determining where to act on this continuum in any situation, you should take four factors into account. They can be seen as restraining factors, holding you back from delegating as fully as you would like. Therefore they need to be kept under constant review.

Confidence in subordinates
You are more likely to delegate if you feel that you can trust your subordinates. That involves a judgement on their professional competence and personal qualities. Able and well-motivated subordinates can obviously take the responsibility you give them; indeed, they will be frustrated if real responsibility and authority is not delegated to them.

The dangers to avoid are over-optimism and over-pessimism about any particular person. We all have our limitations. Some will do an adequate job, with little risk of anything contrary happening. Others need to work in harness with you. The best people are capable, sensible and well-informed, they fully understand the company's objectives and policies and appreciate the possible consequences of mistakes or errors.

For the chief executive or for a leader of equivalent level, delegation should be a way of life, not an optional extra. If he is to make it so, it follows that he must know key subordinates — and potential ones — exceptionally well. Therefore all systems of organisation which divorce him from the people around him or immediately below him must be counter-productive. How can you acquire and maintain that level of knowledge about people? For many good leaders it is a matter of intuition. But intuition can be a misleading guide. You need to spend time working with people, talking about them, observing them and reflecting on them until you form a sure judgement of how far you can delegate to them. And that degree may vary according to the particular decision, task or function which you wish to devolve.

Time available

As a general principle the more you share decisions with others the more time it takes. The very time taken to explain and check understanding, providing sufficient information for the other person to act, may not be yours to give. Crises, where time is necessarily short (and where sometimes life-and-death is involved), do not favour the delegation of decisions, although paradoxically it is often then that having the capacity to delegate all but the most important activities can be most valuable.

Impact on the future

The increased demands on your time should compel you to set priorities and delegate "whatever is time-consuming and not important", as one chief executive put it. The time/importance ratio is worth bearing in mind. You do not want to spend large chunks of time on the least important aspects of your job — and very little time on the big issues.

The natural candidates for delegation are therefore the more routine or administrative parts of your job. It is a mistake, however, to think that you can delegate *all* administration and concentrate solely on leadership. For organising is one of the key functions of a leader. Routine may not be the most enjoyable part of your job, but in every vocation there is an element of toil. Accept the inevitable but essential attention to routine matters and their meticulous implementation.

At the higher levels of leadership, however, you must at all costs avoid getting over-involved in administration. The head of a large chemical company had the right idea when he explained, "I delegate everything that can be defined. This leaves me with score-keeping on jobs that have been delegated and with freedom to spend most time planning opportunities that lie ahead. As soon as they are defined, they will be delegated. My practice has been to select jobs I know best and could supervise most easily and delegate them first. Then as soon as the next job was defined and we could afford staff, it was delegated."

In any position of responsibility it is vital to keep reviewing your present activities in order to see if any of them are ripe for delegation. "I ask myself if anyone else can handle the problem," a managing director told me. "If so, it gets delegated. I am left with decisions no one else is in a position to make and follow up."

Novelty of situation

Among wise senior managers there is a wariness about delegating in areas where the company has insufficient experience to have formulated some guidelines for action. You should expect to hesitate longer before you delegate where the situation is so novel as to be uncharted. For example, negotiations regarding mergers and acquisitions could well fall into this category. It is the nature and delicacy of the assignment — not its complexity — which may make you feel that you must handle it yourself. Where there is a lack of definition, and much uncertainty, coupled with potential major consequences for good or ill on the profitability or development of the organisation, do not delegate the matter to anyone else. Being free for such challenges or opportunities is an essential part of your job.

The primary purpose of delegation is to enable the organisation to be effective, which it cannot be if it is a one-man-band.

The right approach is to assign tasks or functions to others though you remain immediately or ultimately accountable. The measure of authority necessary to perform has to be given too, subject to the degree of control (Fig. 10.2) which you agree with the subordinate. But delegation is also a powerful tool for developing the confidence and abilities of subordinates: it helps them to grow in stature. The art is to delegate just beyond the present capacity of a person, so that they are fully stretched. "I use delegation as a powerful motivational weapon," said a marketing director.

Obviously there is a balance to be struck here between the needs of the company and the development needs of the individual. Wild horses should not be given their heads. Many senior managers can identify with the chairman of an Australian mining company who wrote: "I took over from two successful chairmen who had left too much to others — maybe because of outside interests. The process of curtailing powers and functions already engaged in has been difficult. My basis for delegation is to ensure that I am not landed with major unforeseen consequences."

Many managers in industry and their equivalents in other organisations just cannot bring themselves to delegate more. They want to do everything themselves. If there is a problem to be solved, they must solve it. They do not delegate because they do not *want* to delegate. Often they are workaholics, who have risen by sheer hardwork. Trouble starts when such people are promoted to the level of their incompetence. Large organisations soon lose momentum when there is a poor delegator at the helm and all large decisions — and even relatively minor ones — have to be taken by the head person alone.

The following case study illustrates these points. What are strengths in any manager — the ability to work hard and the willingness to accept responsibility — can become failings unless balanced by other attributes. The admiral who reverts to being a glorified gunnery lieutenant is a familiar type in all organisations. He works non-stop; details attract him like iron filings to a magnet. But people interpret his behaviour as lack of trust in them. Certainly such a person does not develop a management team or grow worthy successors.

CASE STUDY OF A BAD DELEGATOR AT WORK

'Those dear devoted blockheads steamed steadfastly on through the night. They would have died for Jellicoe. But they would not send him a signal.' So John Winton's biography* of Admiral of the Fleet Earl Jellicoe describes the Grand Fleet captains on that confused night off Jutland on 31 May 1916. They had just fought a bloody but inconclusive action against the German High Seas Fleet and looked forward to another — perhaps a glorious Trafalgar — next day.

But it was not to be. Though the enemy had been sighted many times in the night nobody told Jellicoe in time. At dawn, the North Sea was empty. It was John Jellicoe who had to bear the brunt of the nation's disappointment.

Favoured by Admiral Lord Fisher, who had 'heavenly feelings' about his protégé as 'the future Nelson', Jellicoe had been appointed over the heads of 20 more senior admirals. In 1911 Admiral Sir Francis Bridgeman, whose promotion to First Sea Lord from Commander-in-Chief Home Fleet gave Jellicoe his chance, wrote to Fisher:

'Directly I go, up he comes automatically to command of the 2nd Division (Second-in-Command of the Home Fleet) and a splendid opportunity for him! He has had no experience of fleet work on a big scale, and is so extremely anxious about the work on it, that he really does too much. He must learn to work his captains and his staff more, and himself less! At present he puts himself in the position of, say, a glorified gunnery lieutenant. This will not do when he gets with a big fleet. He must trust his staff and captains, and if they don't fit, he must kick them out! I am sure you will agree with me on this view, and I wish, if you get the opportunity, you would drop him a hint. He would take it from you, but perhaps not from me.'

This was a shrewd summary of Jellicoe's most serious fault: his unwillingness to delegate. Although Fisher must have had opportunities to help Jellicoe, he does not seem to have taken them. One of Jellicoe's great flaws remained his inability to delegate. Promoted to be First Sea Lord in 1917, Jellicoe was a sad sight. This dedicated and gifted man gradually deteriorated under the strain of overwork, weariness, irritation with politicians and poor health. On Christmas Eve that year Jellicoe was summarily dismissed from his post.

Jellicoe (Michael Joseph, 1983)

DEVELOPING YOUR SKILLS AS A DELEGATOR

Delegation is an art in the sense that it requires considerable skill to do it well. Just as artistry transcends craftsmanship so true delegation rises above the communication skills needed to allocate tasks to others: both parties feel by intuition that it is right; the creative dimension in some form or another is there. Start with the basic skills and after considerable experience delegation will become second nature to you. The following table should help:

SKILL	NOTES
Selecting the right staff	'There are no bad soldiers — only bad officers.' It is no excuse to blame failure on the quality of your staff. You chose or accepted them. If they are too incompetent or unwilling to do the job even with training you should have got rid of them. Selecting the right people is the foundation of delegation.
Training and developing the individual	However high the potential of your key staff — those to whom you wish to delegate — they will need training. Remember the training cycle: 1. Demonstrate job with delegate alongside 2. Get feedback and comment from him or her 3. Get delegate to do job and observe 4. Delegate does job on own — delegator available to answer questions 5. Delegate does job and reports back on completion Start with small routine tasks and build up to challenging tasks as confidence on both sides grows.

Briefing and checking understanding	Both the training process and subsequent delegation requires considerable two-way communication skills on both parts. What is being delegated must be clearly defined; the authority to do it must be spelt out. Others involved also need to be informed. Check understanding. Make sure the person knows the wider context: company aims and policies. Then he will know why it has to be done and how.
Standing back and supporting	Resist temptations to get involved. Do not rush in and countermand a subordinate's orders. If he comes to you try not to provide the answers but help him to find them. For your aim is to develop the initiative of the subordinate. Then he can cope with problems, including those caused by his actions, as well as you have done in the past.
Controlling in a sensible and sensitive way	No one likes to feel that there is no rope connecting them to the anchor. Check progress at agreed points (see Fig. 10.2). Remember always that abdication is not the name of the game. Control is the essence of delegation.

Fig. 10.3   *Skills of Delegation*

If you are the delegator it is always helpful to put yourself mentally into the shoes of the delegate. Remember these words of a manager looking back on his early days in an insurance company:

"At the end of a long day when I rose from my chair there were times when I used to kick the wastepaper basket under the desk just to relieve my frustration. As I went off home to an examination syllabus in which at least I was master of my own fate I would mutter my prayer to the departmental management:

'Tell me what you want me to do and why
Then let me get on with it
If I make a mess of it kick me hard
So I know where I went wrong
BUT DON'T FUSS'

From the delegate's point of view a delegator who fusses continually is a nightmare. Needless bustle or excitement, a state of agitation especially over details and an undue concern for niceties — the hallmark of a fussy nature — often go hand-in-hand with the kind of person who tends to be irritable and easily upset. Winston Churchill's successor as Prime Minister, Anthony Eden, was a fussy man in this sense. He found it difficult to delegate beyond the ways the system required. If he did so he was on the telephone to the unfortunate minister at all hours of the day and night, restlessly busy over what appeared to any competent subordinate to be mere trifles. He certainly lacked an even temper. No wonder that Churchill, on the eve of his resignation, concluded that Eden was not up to the job of being Prime Minister. But it was then too late.

The crucial importance of creating and sustaining a climate of trust in modern organisations should now be clear. Certainly delegation cannot work properly unless there is mutual trust, founded on personal and professional integrity. Trust is the oxygen of human relationships. Of course you must earn trust by your abilities and contribution, your reliability and trust-worthiness. But trust has still to be given to you as well, and not withheld for wrong reasons.

'Confidence begets confidence,' says an old Roman proverb. Delegation as a gift of trust will generate an answering trust. It will also generate self-confidence in the delegate. Therefore it is an important leadership act towards creating a climate of trust in any organisation. It is worth remembering that people are often better than they think they are and will always respond to a challenge — if it comes from the right source.

Once trust is tarnished it is hard to restore it to its original glow. Therefore do your best to keep it bright. The best way to do this is to stick always to the truth, for truth and trust are sisters. A senior colleague said of Lord Thomson: "his most memorable quality was his instinctive habit of telling the truth. His strength, which was very great, particularly in dark moments, made him enjoy truth when another man would have found illusion more comfortable. He always faced reality and he always believed that he could do good business in terms of the reality that he faced." Such integrity is the golden quality of leadership.

CASE STUDY OF A GOOD DELEGATOR AT WORK

Lord Thomson of Fleet knew how to delegate. In this extract from *Long After I Was Sixty,* his autobiography, he describes his philosophy concerning delegation and how he put it into practice:

'We had been given fair warning about the need for diversification and in Thomson Publications we did not appear to waste any time about it . . . we saw Gordon Brunton off to Australia to have a look at some trade and technical periodicals. I remember he came to see me before leaving.

"How do you want me to handle it?" He was still a new boy after all. "Would you like a survey by telex or to wait till I get back and report to you?"

"You will find half a million available at the bank," I said. "If you see anything worth buying, buy it."

This was the way I invariably trusted my executives. I believed they could do most things as well as I could, if not better, and I always avoided the mistake of kidding myself to the contrary . . . A man must not only know how to choose his executives, he must know how to delegate authority. Lack of this ability shows not only a lack of trust in the individuals themselves but a failure to trust and back one's own judgement. Many of the business failures I have known about throughout my life have come about through this. A man who cannot delegate to others finds himself without the time or energy to concentrate on essential problems. Nor will he be able to take the kind of decisions that are active, immediate and effective. I had also found that it paid to give an executive that confidence right at the start of his career with me.

Gordon was quickly successful in Australia, and bought for us a group of the right kind of periodicals . . .'

Delegation, then, involves a calculated risk. Rational management practice quite properly tries to reduce the margin of risk in decision. There is nothing intrinsically meritorious in taking risks for their own sake. But reducing the margin of risk too slavishly may strengthen the centralizing forces upwards and further the bureaucratic tendencies in large organisations. The true delegator accepts the risk of delegation and its consequences because the alternative would in the long-run be most costly and damaging.

You may wonder how Thomson would have reacted if Brunton had failed in Austalia. Later in the book there is a story which suggests a possible answer. The editor of a leading

British newspaper under Brunton was offered what appeared
to be Benito Mussolini's diaries. After a six-figure payment
had been made some research had established beyond doubt
that the diaries were forgeries. Thomson recalled:

> 'I was in Gordon's room, asking "What is the news?" when he
> told me. It was a substantial sum that had flown with the confi-
> dence men. Gordon recalls that I then asked: "How much
> would we have made if the diaries had turned out to be
> genuine?"
>
> He told me — It would have been the publishing coup of the
> century.
>
> "Well," I said, "it was worth taking the chance."
>
> I then asked him if he would have someone look into my
> driver being paid overtime for taking me home in the evening.
> Was that necessary and right?'

It is interesting to speculate what Thomson would have
said (had he still been alive and owned *The Sunday Times*)
in 1983, when they repeated this same mistake over the
so-called Hitler diaries . . .

Unlike many heads of organisations, Thomson resisted
the temptation to become a back-seat driver. Self-discipline was always at his command. Decisions, major as well
as minor, were left to those he trusted. His chief executives, Gordon Brunton in London and others close to
him, felt a sense of purpose in belonging to the Thomson
Organisation, though some of them could have moved to
more financially rewarding posts; he was not a lavish em-
ployer. As we have seen, he stood by them even when, as
sometimes happened, their decisions turned out to be
wrong — provided they were wrong for the right reasons.
Then no word of reproach came from him.

A true entrepreneurial leader will expect others to act
like entrepreneurs and back them up if the risks do not
come off. He spreads the belief that to a large extent you
can make your own luck. "My idea of luck," said Lord
Thomson, "is that it is an opportunity seized."

Because he delegated, Thomson could always find
time, in the midst of heavy preoccupations and crises, to
consider lesser topics, and to switch his mind to an
altogether different perspective.

Lastly, through delegation Thomson grew managers of stature. Sir Gordon Brunton became Chairman of the International Thomson Organisation in his place, and in his turn proved to be an outstanding business leader.

KEY POINTS

● Delegation begins with a deep sense of the value and limits of your own time. From that stems a strong desire to focus on priorities — the work that only you can do — and to delegate the rest. That will leave you free to think, plan and act effectively.

● Delegation is not abdication. Some degree of control needs to be maintained. The more trustworthy the subordinate the less that will be.

● Managers often complain that they are running out of time when their subordinates are running out of work.

● Delegating the more routine or predictable parts of your job is only the first step. Giving people power to make decisions and to act in your place within a given sphere is the next one. That is not always easy. It requires courage, judgement and faith in others because you remain accountable for what they do.

● Exceptional tasks — those which are absolutely vital and which only you can be sure will be done in time and the required standards — shouldn't be delegated. Nor should those where confidentiality or particular sensitivity is essential. The new, vague or ill-defined task may not be suitable for delegation either, for the subordinates will waste too much time and effort trying to decide how to proceed.

● You should delegate some of your 'positional' authority to your subordinate, matching the task you have given him. But he — like you — will have to rely more on the authority of knowledge and the authority of personality to get things done. Make sure you increase his knowledge and develop his confidence.

● Delegation is a great motivator: it enriches jobs, improves performance and raises morale.

> *'You will never have so much authority as when you begin to give it away.'*

11. Making Use of Committed Time

Glass bottles and cardboard boxes can be recycled. Why not time? Of course time is not like these resources in most respects. But you can recover some committed time from the scrap heap, the destination of those scraps and margins which are left over when a job doesn't quite fit the time available for it.

Committed time is time given over to specific purposes. Things we have to do and places we have to be: these take up much of our time. The aim of this chapter is to suggest some ideas about using off-cuts of time during these committed periods.

In many such situations there is some time when you are not actually doing what you have committed the time for: spare minutes or even hours when you're waiting or not fully occupied. For example, the person you are meeting may be late or the car isn't ready after a service at the garage and you have to sit in the reception office twiddling your thumbs. Or the dentist is running behind his schedule, leaving you contemplating a pile of rather weary-looking magazines. If you are a master of the art of time management you will make some constructive use of these potentially wasted minutes.

For instance, this is an age of travel. You may be travelling constantly. Travel provides many opportunities for saving time. Waiting at airports or stations can be seen as a necessary

evil. Or you can turn it to good ends and write a letter or read a
book. Become a wait-watcher!

Redeeming committed time is a daily challenge. Look upon
it as such. Imagine that the system will be playing against you;
everything will conspire to make you waste time. See if you can
cheat the system. Snatch some small victories today.

DAILY ROUTINES

Sometimes you can put time committed to routine daily
essentials to a second use. Most actions repeated daily, such as
walking, become habitual. Your unconscious mind, which is
like a personal computer in this respect, takes over and runs
the activity. Your mind is more-or-less free to attend to other
things. Therefore time spent on daily routines can often be the
first place to look.

Take getting dressed each day as an example. A pure efficiency expert would get out his stopwatch and ensure that you
spend the minimum amount of time on this daily routine. But
you may *like* dressing. Or you may want to do it in a relatively
leisurely way so that you can think about other things. One
friend of mine, working towards a business degree, records
notes on to a cassette tape recorder and plays them back while
dressing each morning. Another friend's wife is using the same
method to brush up her Italian before going on holiday.

So it is with shaving. An efficiency expert would make you
use two shaving brushes, one in each hand, or persuade you to
use an electric shaver. But the one-brush man has time to
think. Shaving time is remarkably productive in ideas.

Daily exercise is another routine with time-use potential.
One author of phenomenal best-sellers has a reading stand on
his exercise bicycle. Lesser spirits watch television as they exercise on this modern version of the ancient treadmill.

If I can air a personal preference, breakfast ought to be
eaten in complete silence. That happy rule certainly prevailed
in the Scots Guards officers' mess in which I spent some of my
national service days. Places were laid some distance apart in
order to inhibit any attempt at conversation. On my first day I
made the mistake of saying a cheery "Good morning" to a
senior major. "Good morning, good morning, good morning,"

he growled back, not glancing up from his copy of *The Times*, "Now let that last you for the rest of the week."

Meal times illustrate the theme of this chapter perfectly. The primary use of a meal time is to eat and drink. Yet from time immemorial human beings have made meals social occasions, gathering with families and friends to converse together. It is perhaps the oldest and most familiar example of using committed time in a secondary way.

In monasteries and on religious retreats where meals are still eaten in silence, a lector or reader reads aloud passages from edifying books. If the extracts are well-chosen that can be a valuable exercise in getting two benefits for the price of one. A home alternative, assuming the absence of chattering children, would be to have the occasional meal when books can be read in silence at the table. With this end in mind it is worth acquiring or making a reading stand.

After meals comes washing the dishes. The obvious time-saver here is to buy a dish-washer, although with one, two or three people living under a roof that may not save a great deal of time. If for one reason or another you are still committed to washing the dishes by hand, don't despair. Because it is a practical and mindless activity, but one which somehow satisfies your conscience that you are *doing* something, your mind can take wings. Sir Alistair Pilkington is said to have had the key idea which led to the invention of float glass while watching soap in the kitchen sink. Agatha Christie once declared: "The best time for planning a book is when you're doing the dishes."

REDEEMING COMMITTED TIME

In one of his letters of advice to his son, dated 11 December 1747, Lord Chesterfield recalled:

'I knew a gentleman who was so good a manager of his time that he would not even lose that small portion of it which the calls of nature obliged him to pass in the necessary house; but gradually went through all the Latin poets in those moments. He bought, for example, a common edition of Horace, of which he tore off gradually a couple of pages, read them first, then sent them down a sacrifice to Cloacine; this was so much time fairly gained.'

Other physical activities, especially if they are more-or-less habitual, can also serve in the same way as washing the dishes. Bathing, walking, driving, riding a bicycle and gardening are all times when creative people report having ideas or making decisions. Tennyson had so many ideas while bathing that he had a special boiler installed in his house, so that he could take hot baths at any time of the day. It is as if the depth mind has done its work on a problem, like a natural computer, and now answers, solutions or choices are being printed out on the tape of consciousness.

Scores of people have experienced these creative breakthroughs of intuitions while engaged in daily routines or just relaxing by doing something with their hands or walking. A British Nobel prize winner, Dr Godfrey Hounsfield, made the crucial breakthrough which led to the development of the body scanner while walking the Cumbrian fells. "I'm very keen on rambling," he said later. "It's a time when things come to one, I find."

WAITING TIME

Another type of committed time already mentioned is waiting time. For most people it is simply a write-off. With a little planning and resolve, however, you can squeeze all sorts of activities into the minutes you spend waiting for the hairdresser or doctor. You can plan tomorrow's work, write a letter or pay a bill. You can even meditate or reflect in the way recommended in the following chapter.

Waiting time, for instance in an airport lounge, gives you some bonus minutes of solitude if not silence. Be prepared for them by having the right frame of mind. As Goethe said, "Solitude is a wonderful thing when one is at peace with oneself and when there is a definite task to be accomplished."

TRAVEL TIME

Travelling time has already been mentioned as a prime target. As a schoolboy I commuted to London every day for five years, a journey of an hour each morning and evening. I learnt then the value of travelling time, for most of the required homework could be done on the train.

Arnold Bennett, writing in 1907, pictured the plight of the typical commuter. 'He walks to the station in a condition of mental coma. Arrived there, he usually has to wait for the train. On hundreds of suburban stations every morning you see men calmly strolling up and down platforms while railway companies unblushingly rob them of time, which is more than money. Hundreds of thousands of hours are thus lost every day simply because my typical man thinks so little of time that it has never occurred to him to take quite easy precautions against the risk of its loss.'

Reading newspapers on trains struck Bennett as a major time-waster. Although he read five English and two French dailies he objected to reading newspapers in the morning train. 'Newspapers are produced with rapidity, to be read with rapidity. There is no place in my daily programme for newspapers. I read them as I may in odd moments. But I do read them. The idea of devoting to them thirty or forty minutes of wonderful solitude is to me repugnant. I cannot possibly allow you to scatter priceless pearls of time with such Oriental lavishness. You are not the Shah of time. No newspaper reading in trains!'

Anthony Trollope achieved his prodigious output as a novelist by writing his book on trains. As an employee of the General Post Office he was obliged to travel widely around the country over a period of years, and he put his time on trains to good use.

Long air flights can provide similar opportunities. All air travel tends to be fragmented. Short-haul flights may save time in one way, but it is harder to get any work done on them. At airports, however, you will usually find some waiting time available after checking-in.

Many managers remain addicted to driving themselves to work. Driving demands concentration. Therefore it is a dead loss as far as redeeming committed time is concerned, unless you include listening to taped music under that heading. The best place for your car is in the garage unless you really have to use it to get to work.

TRAVELLING MAN

Sir Terence Beckett, a leading British industrialist, believes in train travel:

'You have a table in front of you and you can spread your papers out and really get on with the job in a much better way than with you knees under your chin in a car or, worse still, with your elbows clamped to your sides in an aircraft.

I look forward to train journeys with real pleasure. By air, your air travel time is only a small part of the total. It's getting to the airport, hanging about and all the rest of it. With rail you spend your time on the train, not constantly sprinting from one place to another.'

Valuing his interludes of privacy, Sir Terence does not approve of the new telephones on trains. Nor does he ever take a secretary along.

'To me, one of the great pleasures of going by train is that they can't get you on the phone . . . The chief advantage is to get away from them all and to get on with it yourself. I don't get enough time to do that.

You can start thinking about things that in a busy life — and that's what mine has been for all my career — you don't get the chance to think about. You do get some very good ideas as a result, especially on people and organisation that you've really meant to think about for quite some time. When you come back you make decisions that perhaps you ought to have made before. A train journey is almost structuring in, if you like, a bit of time to think.'

TELEVISION

When Arnold Bennett's typical commuter arrived home he had no radio or television to tempt him. An hour or so after getting back 'you feel as if you could sit up and take a little nourishment. And you do. Then you smoke, seriously; you see friends; you potter; you play cards; you flirt with a book; you note that old age is creeping on; you take a stroll; you caress the piano . . . By Jove! a quarter past eleven. Time to think about going to bed!'

Radio and, more so, television have revolutionized that Edwardian evening. Many people now look upon the evening as time committed to television. I am a keen watcher of television. I am obliged to mention this personal fact lest I should be accused of a prejudice against television when I say that committing the whole evening to it is a terrible waste of time.

The American idea of television is becoming universal. It is primarily that television will create and serve a nation or world of consumers. To suit the advertisers every home must have two or more television sets which are on continuously day and night, showing programmes that are accessible to all viewers and always alluring. Dynamic visual imagery therefore takes precedence over language. Everything must be packaged as entertainment. An audience engaging in serious thought might not pay enough attention to the commercials. Indeed a thinking audience may see little difference between most of the programmes and the commercials.

Americans now watch an average of eight hours of amusing television *each day*. During his lifetime the typical American will see approximately 2,000,000 relentlessly entertaining commercials, at the rate of 1,000 a week. According to a recent estimate, some 60 million Americans — almost one-third of the entire population — could be classified as illiterate. Almost as many again may be aliterate (people who can read but don't). "Welcome to the Age of Television — Have a wonderful time."

What can you do about it? You can try budgeting the time you spend watching television and choose your programmes accordingly. If the television set is on for one reason or another see if you can do something else, like reading a book. Let your subconscious mind filter the programme for you, so that you glance up or take notice when something interesting is going on. The invention of the remote-control box is an invaluable aid here: all the commercials, for example, can be shown without sound.

The television advertisers are out to get your time. Can you afford to deliver them three hours of it every evening for the rest of your life?

KEY POINTS

- You have to commit time, but not all committed time is used. Become aware of time as a piece of cloth that you are constantly cutting into shape. Pick up the off-cuts, the pieces of marginal time, and make use of them.

- Review your daily routines. Simply because they are routines — habitual and settled ways of proceeding — you may find that your mind could be active if stimulated by, for example, a tape recorder.

- Waiting time, be it long or short, can be a positive opportunity rather than a negative time-drag. Become a wait-watcher!

- When choosing the most time-effective method of travel take into account the quality and quantity of the work you will be able to do on the journey.

- Review the amount of time you devote to watching television. If necessary cut down on quantity. Also, for most programmes, reduce the quality of your attention. You can do something else while half-watching, like a grandmother knitting while listening to the radio.

'We all find time to do what we really want to do.'

12. On Health and Holidays

You may think it strange to find a chapter on health and holidays in a book on time management. What is the connection between the subjects? Why include it?

There is one obvious reason; if you are ill it is an interruption to what you are doing. Time may not be exactly wasted while you are recuperating, but it is certainly channelled into another use. A reasonable, positive and effective interest in your health is like taking out an insurance policy against illness which threatens to rob you of time that you would rather spend in some other way. Prevention is better than cure.

A deeper reason, however, concerns the *quality* of your time. Most books on time management concern themselves solely with the quantity of time you have available to you. They seek to persuade you to work longer hours by getting up earlier and by cutting out distractions or time-wasters. They frighten you with constant reminders of how little time is left. But they seldom address themselves to the fundamental issue: how can you increase the *quality* of your time? The aim of this chapter is to answer that question.

Imagine that work — your expenditure of energy and time in purposeful activity — is like a football match. What happens off the field, before the whistle blows, is vitally important to the outcome of the match. Are the players fit? Are they relaxed and confident? If their physical fitness and mental condition, especially their morale, is not good they are unlikely to produce high quality football. So it is with you. However knowledgeable you are about the techniques of time management you will not gain the most from your time — the essence of the art — unless you are feeling physically and mentally fit. How can that be achieved?

YOUR ENERGY BALANCE

One of the major foundations of this book has been the analogy of time to money. You could apply the same metaphor to energy. But there is an important difference. Nature is capricious. Everyone is born potentially with the same amount of time; energy comes in variable quantities. You have a quota of it. Wisely used it can last you a lifetime.

In this respect energy does compare to a bank balance. Your money could be left to stagnate. Or you could add regular sums to it, building up your capital over the years. In many ways it's possible to be fitter in the fifties than at forty. You can be reasonably energetic well into your eighties, given some luck and if you have invested in your energy capital.

What is your energy? It is best defined as power expended or capable of being transformed into work. Work, of course, is not necessarily the same as paid employment. Energy shows itself in vigorous action, forceful utterance, strenuous exertion and vitality.

Tycoons, like all others who have a passion for work, necessarily need an extraordinary amount of energy to fuel their furnaces. Many a talented young manager has failed to become a tycoon — a businessman of exceptional wealth and power — simply because he wasn't built to take the grind. "It becomes clear pretty soon if you can't do the job," said one entrepreneur to me. Another successful businessman made the same point: "Thoroughbreds are bred to race. It's the same with people. It's something that's inborn."

Thoroughbreds, like all other kinds of work horse, have to sleep, eat and exercise. The reservoir of your energy is fed directly from these three sources. Here is some commonsense advice under those three headings.

GET ENOUGH SLEEP

'Sleep that knits up the ravell'd sleeve of care,
The death of each day's life, sore labour's bath,
Balm of hurt minds, great nature's second course,
Chief nourisher in life's feast . . .'

Shakespeare's words in *Macbeth* capture both the mystery and the properties of sleep. No one understands fully why we must sleep and what happens in sleep. But it is clear that sleep is essential for our physical and mental wellbeing. In other words, sleep conserves and restores our energy.

Individuals vary as to how much sleep they need. Some are Napoleons who can manage on as little as three hours a night. (But here you should be cautious before accepting the stories that gather around charismatic leaders, emphasizing their power and energy. For example, the Mussolini myth portrayed him as a man of enormous energy, needing very little sleep. In fact, he slept as long as a normal person.) Most people can occasionally manage on three hours sleep a night: it is the average requirement you should look at. That usually becomes less as we grow older.

It is important to discover roughly how much sleep you need each night and keep to it. For example, Archbishop William Temple, a man of wide-ranging interests and phenomenal accomplishment, was an exceptionally good manager of time. From his religious upbringing in childhood he had imbibed the idea that it was sinful to waste time. In between official functions and in various spare moments he composed books and wrote letters. At the height of the Second World War, when he was Archbishop of Canterbury, he ended one letter — 'I must stop now and get to bed, as I am writing out of my sleep.' Doing anything 'out of your sleep' is to be avoided if at all possible.

Margaret Thatcher, who found that she could exist on very little sleep each night, had still had to learn the same lesson. She decided in 1984 to burn less midnight oil and to restrict the amount of work she did in the small hours of the morning. But Mrs. Thatcher whose voracious appetite for work and attention to detail is second to none, maintained her workload by spending more time studying her papers before breakfast. The change stemmed in part from concern at the strain on her eyes from too much late-night reading. "I now find it far better to apply a fresh mind in the morning rather than reading long hours into the night," she said.

Some people are plagued with insomnia. The first remedy is to remember first that we all sleep more than we think we do. So do not worry about lack of sleep. Secondly, get up and do something. Or, if you wake early, lie in bed and apply your mind to a work problem. You will recall that this is the principle of moonlighting (see p74).

If it suits you, take cat naps during the day (although this isn't advisable if you are not sleeping well at night). Edison and Einstein both made a nap part of their daily routine. Churchill, Truman, Eisenhower, and Kennedy are examples of political leaders who used naps as means of maintaining their energy level and coping with the pressures of high office.

Check yourself against the following questions:

● Do you know how many hours sleep you need to average each night?

● Have you suffered from insomnia at some time in the last six months? If so, what were the causes?

● Do you regularly go to bed too late at night, leaving yourself tired and irritable in the mornings?

● Have you tried taking cat naps during the day?

● Are you over-sleeping? Could you now manage with an hour's less sleep a night?

COMMONSENSE DIET

Today we are bombarded with advice from all sides on the subject of what to eat and drink. Many of these shots of advice fail to hit their target. For example, the Western world is now well aware that the habit of smoking can give you lung cancer, not to mention heart disease. The advice to refrain from smoking is still ignored by a significant part of the population.

One difficulty in the diet field is that experts change their minds. Once they told us firmly to avoid potatoes and bread: these foods contained fattening carbohydrates. Now potatoes, especially baked ones, and bread, especially of the brown wholemeal variety, are in favour. They contain, for instance, useful quantities of fibre. Faced with these sometimes discordant messages you should follow three rules:

1. Resolve now whether basically you are the kind of person who lives to eat, or one who eats to live. If you are of the second kind, read on. If you live to eat — gourmet or glutton — then no advice on diet is worth reading — your values are different.
2. Watch out for any consensus among dieticians. For example, there is a clear agreement in favour of a balanced diet including vegetables, fruit, fish and bread. A consensus is emerging against too much sucrose, especially in the form of white sugar. Common sense, aided by a little instruction from the experts, is your best guide.
3. Remember the golden rule: *nothing in excess.* Cream, butter, sugar, alcohol and the other suspect foods are all right if taken in moderation or occasionally. Conversely, consuming all the products of a health food shop immoderately will do your digestive system no good.

TAKE EXERCISE

Exercise is almost as contentious a field as diet. But the same basic principles apply. First, you must establish your priorities. If you are too busy to exercise you are too busy. For exercise generates energy, despite consuming it in the short term. You shouldn't be living in order to exercise, like some fanatics, but taking exercise in order to live more fully.

The second rule of looking for the consensus points among the experts is easy to apply. They all approve of such exercises as tennis, golf, walking, swimming or cycling: activities which make you breathe deeply and increase your heartrate. The heart is a muscle which likes exercise. The respiratory and digestive systems are fellow beneficiaries when you walk briskly, swim or cycle. Therefore you would be wise to find some form or exercise which you enjoy and invest some time in doing it two or three times a week. It will both increase your efficiency and help you relax.

The third rule — nothing in excess — applies to the craze for jogging. Done immoderately on hard surfaces this can lead to damaged knees, ankles and backs. According to some experts jogging is also as addictive as coffee or heroin, as it releases brain chemicals known as endorphins designed for time of body crisis, giving the jogger a 'lift' without which he becomes depressed. Such victims of jogging are classic examples of overdrawn energy bank balances.

Some people indulge in sudden bursts of exercise on the squash court, a potentially fatal experience for the unfit business executive. If you are taking up vigorous exercise it is wise to warm up first.

Regularity is important. Exercising three or four times a week gradually brings the heartrate up. Brisk walking is always good exercise, so is gardening or anything else that involves stretching arms and legs. It is important to move the body and use the muscles in this way, for that keeps your body supple. Enjoy whatever form of exercise you choose — then you will keep on doing it.

"It is a fact," said Max Beerbohm, "that not once in my life have I gone for a walk." He could not have known what he was missing! Walking has much to commend it as a form of exercise. You can do it anywhere and you do not need any special clothes or equipment.

Apart from perhaps setting aside some time for walking in the countryside at weekends you can also find opportunities for energetic walking each working day. It is the same principle as walking up or down the stairs rather than taking the lift — the value of the extra exercise is worth the expenditure of a little more time, for exercise is the vital principle of health and you ignore it at your peril.

"Yes, yes," you say, "but I haven't got time to take exercise in the regular way you are recommending. I am too busy tackling all those goals and objectives I have identified as a result of reading your book."

If that is what you are feeling it may be worth thinking

about the answer Olympic gold medallist Sebastian Coe gave to suggestions that intense concentration on athletics may have narrowed his life:

THE PRICE OF FITNESS

I hear a lot of talk about the great sacrifices involved in running, but personally I think it's a matter of organising your time efficiently. I can run in the amount of time most people spend watching television. It's been worked out that the average person spends about three to four hours watching television every night. Well, in one and a half hours I can do a hell of a lot of good work. If that's missing out, it doesn't worry me. If running means not going to night clubs, not drinking excessively and not smoking, that's fine. I don't like that sort of life anyway.

Sebastian Coe

Sebastian Coe broke the 800 metre world record in Oslo in 1979 by this kind of self-discipline. If he could run for ninety minutes a day, surely you and I can exercise a mere ninety minutes a week in order to be fit for daily living.

THE IMPORTANCE OF HOLIDAYS

Don't become a workaholic! Working hard is not the same as working long hours. If you do have to work long hours over a period of time compensate by working less hard when you can. Friends, family and recreation are worth your time. Get your priorities right and maintain them. Symptoms of work addiction include refusal to take a holiday, inability to 'switch off' from thinking about work and a husband or wife, son or daughter who are practically strangers to you. If that is happening to you, you need a holiday.

What constitutes a good holiday is fortunately a personal matter. Ask yourself what was the most memorable holiday you have ever had. Its ingredients — travel, friends, history, food, sun, beaches, mountains, sport or whatever — may be a relative guide when it comes to planning your next one, subject, of course, to the law that variety is the spice of life. With holidays change for change's sake is sometimes a good thing.

If you are a time-conscious business executive or a professional person daily managing your time with care, reflect on J.B. Priestley's definition. "A good holiday," he said, "is one spent among people whose notions of time are vaguer than yours."

Holidays were originally holy-days, extra days apart from Sunday set aside so that people could remember the great events or saints of their religion. Holidays now are both secularized and largely commercialized. Perhaps we need to return to that fundamental idea that holidays are a time for mental and spiritual recreation, not merely for regimenting our bodies with a change of air and diet. For the quality of our time may depend as such on the state of our minds as upon the condition of our bodies.

Leisure hours in the evenings or at weekends are holidays in miniature. Many occupations provide plenty of mental exercise and stimulus. Should your job fall into that category, however, you may yet consider doing things in your leisure hours or during your holidays which will use other parts of your brain, such as learning a language or using a computer. In *Effective Decision Making* (1984) I have given some guidelines for becoming and remaining mentally fit. That is as important as physical fitness, but strangely neglected by the health industry.

PRACTICAL MEDITATION

The fruits of prayer and meditation were exemplified in Archbishop William Temple. Humility, he once said, is "not thinking little of self but in not thinking of self at all." Temple had the highest freedom available to a person, namely the ability to live each day and each hour without fretfulness or anxiety. He once said, very characteristically, "What wears one out is not what one does but what one doesn't do."

In the Christian tradition prayer and meditation are linked. Prayer can be understood by analogy as a familiar conversation with God. The decline in religious belief in the West has led to a rise in the popularity of eastern forms of meditation, which are not linked to the Jewish, Christian or Muslim concept of God.

Theosophy, Yoga and Zen-Buddhism are just three examples of such eastern influence upon western spiritual methods. Only in the last decade or so has meditation been packaged and sold to businessmen by various gurus. A programme which has achieved some popularity is Transcendental Meditation — TM for short. You sit silently for 20 minutes twice a day, eyes closed, letting your mind wander where it will while silently repeating a *mantra*, a Sanskrit word that sounds like nonsense syllables. Practitioners say that it makes you more alert and less tense. Some physical changes, such as altered brainwaves and slower, deeper breathing, are also said to occur.

THE SECRET OF MAHATMA GANDHI

More than any other worker, the leader must lay up and safeguard reserves. Gandhi is a good illustration. He impresses one as being very frail physically. Yet where is there a leader subjected to greater strain? I think I found the secret of his wonderful endurance when I visited him at his Ashram near Ahmedabad. The only day on which I could arrange my crowded programme so as to step off to see him turned out, as I discovered on arrival, to be his day of silence. He graciously invited me in writing to sit with him during the period which terminated shortly after dusk. We then had a memorable conversation under the stars as he lay on his couch in front of his cottage. Among other things I asked him toward the close of our interview to tell what led him to observe a day of silence. He replied that he was so tired of talking and of hearing others talk. He found that in the tremendous pressure upon him he was not only breaking down physically but losing mental freshness and spiritual power, and was in danger of becoming formal, mechanical, and devitalized. He craved quiet for thought and prayer. And so he resolutely observes one day of complete silence each week. He told me that someone had asked him whether he would not break the silence in order to talk with the Viceroy, and he had replied that he would not do so for any person.

Sir Richard Livingstone

As the above passage makes clear, a key factor in all meditation is the need for silence. "Turn aside and listen," says the teacher. "Sometimes you'll hear a quite different voice to those which assail you all day long. Let the babble of the human menagerie die down." Quietness and contemplation go hand in hand. If you wish to meditate your first objective must be to create a time-bounded silence. It may be ten minutes early in the morning or late at night or an hour or two walking by yourself or sitting on a river bank fishing. But the essential point is that you are alone and things are quiet. 'Silence is good medicine for the heart,' says a Chinese proverb.

Although you should not aim to bulldoze your thoughts in any one direction meditation should be a purposeful activity. It is not the same as wasting time, still less killing it. You need to take a thought, an idea or a theme and gradually nibble away at it like a caterpillar on a cabbage leaf.

You could take the theme of this book — or some particular facet of it — as the subject of your meditations for a week. Take any three thoughts, words or phrases from this book. Write them down on plain postcards. Set aside 10 or 15 minutes before breakfast each day, beginning tomorrow.

Some people find it helpful to meditate with a pencil in hand, jotting down any thoughts that come to them. Think of the thought or phrase as a diamond, which you are holding up to the light, looking into hidden flaws or fissure, turning to see each new facet. It is a journey of discovery, in which the ordinary discloses the extraordinary.

At the end of your three meditations, you may at least be more deeply aware of some aspect of time. You may be more conscious of it as a mystery or more grateful for it as an unexpected gift. Meditation is beginning to work for you. No effort; no reward.

So far I have been suggesting that you should meditate in a fairly structured way, selecting a subject and deliberately choosing or creating times when you can be alone and quiet. Meditation can be done in less structured ways.

Perhaps a better name for it would be reflection. Something said to you, some event, a thought-provoking sentence in a book, the changing seasons, the music of family life: any of these may start you thinking. We sometimes picture thinking as a kind of hard labour — mental work that produces a sweat on the brow. And so it can be. But in solitude, relaxing by the fire with a glass, thinking can also be a kind of play: an enjoyable exploration of some vein of meaning in your life. Such reflections may yield you moments of insight or deepen your values or warm your feelings, but even if they do not they are worth entertaining for their own sake. The fruit will come.

Reverie of this kind has been called 'the Sunday of thought'. It is a good idea to spend some time just meditating in this relaxed way about what you are doing in your work at present, even if it is only for a few minutes each day. Walter Bagehot once said, "No great work has ever been produced except after a long interval of still and musing meditation."

TIME TO THINK

At some stage during the day, often during the evening, I make time for an hour's meditation. I sit in an armchair, perhaps with a glass of whisky, and consider what's going to happen tomorrow. I think of what the importance of it all is. I think of family things.

What it does is to put life into perspective. Something which at 10am seemed a terribly worry is no longer a worry when viewed in the context of what life is all about. I think that's why I'm a placid person. For some people a small event can become an obsession. Meditation stops one being constantly impetuous and in politics that's important. Leo Amery first advised me to meditate and now having done it for 16 or 17 years I couldn't do without it.

I never worry about what the future holds in politics. I take things as they come, otherwise there's too much to worry about. First you worry about becoming an MP; then you worry about becoming minister of state; then you worry about becoming secretary of state, chancellor, foreign secretary or prime minister. And when you reach any of those positions you worry about losing them. If you are crazy enough to do that you will not enjoy politics.

Peter Walker

Practical meditation of this kind can change your life. Spiritually you need such times of silence and solitude. Pascal wrote: 'All the troubles of life come upon us because we refuse to sit quietly for a while each day in our rooms.'

COPING WITH STRESS

John Smith is jolted awake by his shrill alarm clock. It took him a long time to get to sleep last night and he still hasn't shaken off his throbbing headache.

He won't be going into work today and his absence, along with that of thousands of others will have been caused by stress.

Stress, defined by the Oxford English Dictionary as simply

pressure or tension, can cause a myriad of conditions from skin disorders, stomach ulcers, high blood pressure and headaches to nervous breakdowns and heart attacks.

Are you suffering from stress? The warning signs include:

- Disturbed sleep
- Constant tiredness
- Incessant worry
- Increased use of alcohol
- Excessive smoking
- Impotence or frigidity
- Over-eating
- Reliance on sleeping pills
- Drugs
- Irritability
- Lack of appetite

- Nausea
- Fainting spells
- Tendency to sweat for no obvious reason
- Insomnia
- Nail-biting
- Nervous 'tics'
- Frequent crying or desire to cry
- Headaches
- Frequent indigestion

Many managers only recognise stress when they or an employee reach a crisis. This may be alcoholic dependence or a nervous breakdown.

Stress symptoms can be friends warning us to re-examine our life-style — the self-diagnosis can be: "I need to take a searching look at myself and my career". What concept do you have of yourself and of the time/change continuum — how much time do you have to change your ways? The need is to develop a philosophy of life which embraces body, mind, spirit, career and relationships.

There are times, however, when stress invades our lives like the sea surging over the natural barriers of sand dunes and man-made sea walls.

Sheila Henderson was looking forward to the New Year. Aged fifty, without children of her own, she had an interesting job working with a group of unemployed young people. Her husband Michael was a senior marketing executive with a large pharmaceutical company. For eight months she had been nursing her mother at home, which she found exhausting. Suddenly, a week before Christmas, her mother suffered another stroke and died in the ambulance taking her to hospital, Sheila holding her hand. As an only child Sheila was hard hit by the loss of her mother. Two days later Michael received a curt note from his new chief executive saying that his services would no longer be required in the New Year. That same evening the police telephoned to say that three of her teenage youth trainees had been involved in a drugs party and had assaulted an elderly woman on a housing estate. The day after her mother's funeral was a Saturday, a day when Michael and Sheila usually played golf. "You go ahead," she said, "and I'll join you later." But in the kitchen after he had left she collapsed with an agonizing pain in her neck. She could hardly move. Doctors eventually diagnosed worn discs and advanced arthritis and told her that there was no cure. Two years later, however, when the causes of stress had eased so did the pain in her neck.

The story of Sheila Henderson illustrates how stress is cumulative. It's not just one situation but continual stress that leads to problems. A relatively minor event, when added to a large existing stress burden, can be the proverbial straw which breaks the camel's back. So if it's feasible, space out your changes as much as you can. Often, however, you won't have control over the kind of events which head the list of stressors: the death of a husband or wife, the death of a parent or child or close friend, a marital separation or parting from someone you love, illness or injury, major changes at work, and the loss of your job. So your objective then is to adapt your response to them.

The onset of serious stress symptoms may not be so sudden and dramatic in your life as in the above case, but the physical signs of pressure, anxiety and depression can be equally worrying. If that is the case the obvious first step is to consult your doctor, to ensure that there is nothing fundamentally wrong. Then you need to follow a seven-point plan to cope with this unwelcome visitor, which covers both external and internal factors.

Sensible time management tackles the twelve most common roots of management stress. Research on 1000 managers in 10 countries (reported in *International Management,* May 1984) has identified these as follows:

1. Time pressures and deadlines
2. Work overload
3. Inadequately trained subordinates
4. Long working hours

5. Attending meetings
6. Demands of work on private and social life
7. Keeping up with new technology
8. Holding beliefs conflicting with those of the organisation
9. Taking work home
10. Lack of power and influence
11. The amount of travel required by work
12. Doing a job below one's level of competence

For one or more of the reasons given above, however, stress can break through your sea defences. What can you do to manage or control it? If you are already experiencing some symptoms of stress here's what to do about it:

1. TAKE ACTION	Regard the symptoms in a positive light, as early warnings. Identify the underlying stress factors and do something about them. For example, if you are unhappy at work take stock and look at other options open to you, such as retraining or applying for a move. Any action is better than brooding. Go for a walk, take some exercise. Smile and respond cheerfully, despite your feelings.
2. EXPRESS YOUR FEELINGS	Avoid isolation. Try to communicate with others. Don't bottle up your feelings. Find a way of expressing your anger and hostility, if that's what you feel. Talking to a friend or spouse might be the answer. Or you may have to seek professional help from a doctor, pastor or counsellor.
3. REVIEW PRIORITIES	Stand back and take a look at your values and priorities. You may be suffering from self-inflicted wounds. A fresh vision of your priorities in life can clear your mind of confusion and stress. Balance work with recreation. Abandon the all-work, no-play ethic.

4. ACCEPT WHAT CANNOT BE CHANGED	Seek the courage to change the things that can be changed and the serenity to accept the things that cannot be changed — and the wisdom to know the difference.
5. PUT YOUR EXPERIENCE TO GOOD USE	Put the negative experience to work in some way or other. Thus you redeem it. That means turning a minus into a plus. For example, use your own suffering to become more sympathetic to others who are going through the mill.
6. CHECK YOUR TIME MANAGE-MENT SKILLS	Don't accept or set yourself unrealistic deadlines. Remember that too tight a programme for the time available is the major cause of management stress. Review all your time management skills where you suspect that you are weak, such as delegation. Allocate more time to your important tasks. Work and act methodically, doing one job at a time.
7. COUNT YOUR BLESSINGS NOT YOUR AFFLICTIONS	Concentrate on the present. Avoid dwelling on past events or future uncertainties. Gratitude is your greatest ally. Make a list now of five things for which you can be truly thankful. In your meditation this week, see if you can add five more blessings to your list.

Fig. 12.1   *Seven Steps to Counter Stress*

Worry is always a potential enemy, especially when you are feeling tired. When it assails you remember Mark Twain's words, "I have known a great many troubles, but most of them never happened."

KEY POINTS

- Conserve your energy and build your health by following sensible guidelines over sleep, diet and holidays. Remember that the golden rule is moderation.

- Practical meditation requires the simple ingredients of silence and solitude. Take some time each day to reflect upon things. You may wish to meditate in the classical sense of feeding upon some truth or value. Or you may like to reflect upon the deeper agenda of the day. Are your priorities right? Are you missing some blessings in disguise?

- Learn to recognise the symptoms of stress and to diagnose the underlying factors. Apply a seven-step strategy for coping with stress if it invades your life: take action; express your feelings; review priorities; accept what cannot be changed; put your experience to good use; check your time management skills; and count your blessings, not your afflictions.

- If you are worried, focus the object of your worry as definitely as possible in the camera of your mind. Ask yourself, "What's the *worst* that could come of this? Can I cope with *that?*" If you can answer those questions, the nagging worry will usually vanish.

- Live one day at a time. You can't change what occurred yesterday. You can make tomorrow better by living well today.

'Lord, there's never enough time for everything.
Help me to do a little less a little better.'

Summary: Ten Steps Towards Better Time Management

- Develop a personal sense of time

- Identify long-term goals

- Make middle-term plans

- Plan the day

- Make best use of your best time

- Organise office work

- Manage meetings

- Delegate effectively

- Make use of committed time

- Manage your health

Appendix A

EXERCISE CHIEF EXECUTIVE

Suggested answer:

1. Ensuring that the organisation has a sense of direction, expressed in clear aims and objectives. (Does the board of directors and senior managers know where the organisation is now in relation to its competitors and markets and where it wants to be in three years' time? Does it have vision?)

2. Establishing a corporate plan, flexible in nature which will lead to the attainment of those aims and objectives.

3. Deciding on priorities — the allocation of money and resources in accordance with aims/objectives and plans.

4. Determining major policies, the ones that will guide the decisions of managers further down the line. Major policies are those which establish or develop the value system to which the company will adhere.

5. Organising, in the sense of determining the basic organisational structure, and selecting/developing the key executives.

6. Developing four or five potential successors in the context of developing a management team.

7. Building relationships with the chairman and board of directors.

8. Forging key external relationships within the industry, with major customers, with the community and with government.

9. Controlling, including the establishment of standards and the monitoring of performance, in order that the organisation achieves its aims and objectives.

Appendix B

The key points made in this book are available on a selection of Filofax loose leaf pages. They provide a reminder of the basic principles outlined in detail in the preceding pages.

A Filofax diary and notebook is the ideal accompaniment to this book. If you are already a user of the Filofax system, you will have discovered that it is the most comprehensive of all loose leaf systems designed to promote personal organisation and time management. Its strength lies in its versatility. No diary could be more flexible or accommodating than the Filofax system. You can select from a very wide range of leaves and assemble them into a system of your choice to meet your own needs and to suit preferences. The Filofax personal system you have created then has the great advantage that you can add to it or subtract pages while maintaining core diary and information sections for regular use.

Filofax products are available in most large towns in the United Kingdom and in many major cities throughout the world. Should you, however, have any difficulty locating an outlet please telephone or write to Filofax plc, mentioning this book and you will be informed about the nearest shops which stock Filofax. The address is:—

> Filofax plc,
> Filofax House,
> Forest Road,
> Ilford, Essex IG6 3HP
> Telephone: 01-501 3911.

Bibliography

Bennett, A.

How to Live on Twenty-Four Hours A Day, New York, Cornerstone Library Edition, 1962.

Bliss, E.C.

Getting Things Done: The ABCs of Time Management, Elm Tree, 1979.

Carlson, S.

Executive Behaviour: A Study of the Work Loads and the Working Methods of Managing Directors, Strombergs, Stockholm, 1951.

Cooper, J.

How to Get More Done in Less Time, Doubleday, 1971.

Douglass, M.E. and D.N.

Manage Your Time, Manage Your Work, Manage Yourself, Amacom, 1980.

Drucker, P.

The Effective Executive, Heinemann, 1967.

Ferner, J.D.

Successful Time Management, John Wiley, 1979.

Januz, L.R. and Jones, S.K.

Time Management for Executives, Sidgwick and Jackson, 1981.

Lakein, A.

How to Get Control of Your Time and Your Life, Gower, 1984.

Landes, D.S.   *Revolution in Time: Clocks and the
                            Making of the Modern World,* Harvard
                            University Press, 1983.

LeBoeuf, M.   *Working Smart,* McGraw-Hill, 1979.

Love, S.F.   *Mastery and Management of Time,*
                            Prentice Hall, 1978.

Oncken, W.   *Managing Management Time,* Prentice
                            Hall, 1984.

McCay, J.T.   *The Management of Time,* Prentice
                            Hall, 1959.

Reynolds, H. and   *Executive Time Management,* Gower,
Tramel, M.E.   1984.

Turla, P. and   *Time Management Made Easy,*
Hawkins, K.L.   Granada, 1985.

Webber, R.A.   *Time and Management,* Van Nostrand,
                            1972.

Index

administration 89
aims 51,58,64,65,121,153
alcohol 141
Alberti, Leon 7
Albery, James 14-15
ambition 40
Amery, Leo 145
anxiety 147
Attlee, Clement 104,109
asking technique 93
athletics 140,141
atomic clocks 4,6
attitude to time 55-56, 64,77,112

Bagehot, Walter 144
Baldwin, Faith 87
banks 9
Beckett, Sir Terence 132
Bennett, Arnold 9,10,11,25,63,
64,130,131,132
Bethlehem Steel Company 61
Black Death 7
booking time 58
books to read (bibliography) 185-8
boredom 4
brain-storming 49,74
Bridgeman, Admiral Sir Francis 119
Brunton, Sir Gordon 123,124,125
budgeting time 1,46,57,62,63,94,133
for meetings 21
business writing 84,85

case studies:
    good delegator 123
    ineffective chairman 20-22
    office mismanager 18-20
    poor delegator 15-18, 119
    procrastinator 13-14
    undirected trainer 22-24
chairman, ineffective 20-22
chairman's role 102-5
    skill enhancement
checklists:
    delegation 17
    managing office time 20
    meetings 21-22
Chesterfield, Lord 29,129
chief executive, exercise 114
    answer 153-4
Christianity 142
Christie, Agatha 129
Churchill, Winston 68,122,138
clarity of expression 84
clocks 6,7,8,11
    atomic 4,6
    mechanical 6,7
    portable 6
Coe, Sebastian 140-141
coiled spring 6
Columbus, Christopher 41

committed time, redeeming
                    127-34,151
    driving 131
    television 132-133,134
    waiting time 130,134
    while travelling
              127,130,131,132,134
committees, formal 21
commuting, 130,132
computers, personal 89
contingency provisions 53
control of subordinates 113,121,125
core mission 23,31
corporate plan 153
creative thinking
    68,69,70,71,72,73,74,75,76,104
crisis 146
council meeting 95,96

daily list 59-61,63,64-65
    check questions 61-62
daily routines,
    second use of 128-130,134
    dishwashing 129,130
    dressing 128
    exercise time 128
    mealtimes 129
    physical activities 130
    shaving 128
data interpretation and analysis 89
day, planning the 55-65
deadlines 18,53,59,94,149
decisions 62,69,95,96,105,123,132
Declaration of Independence 90
delegation 15-18,26,51,59,
                117,119,123,149,151
    art of 111-126
    difficulties of 111-126
    scale 115,117
    seven reasons for not doing 113
    skills 120,121,122
    time/importance ratio 116
    trusting subordinates
        115-116,118,119,122,123,125

what can be delegated 115-118
    what cannot be delegated
                    113-114
depression 147
depth mind 71,72,74,75,76,130
deskmanship 80-81, 90-91
diaries 57-59
diet 138-139,150
dimension of time 4,11
discipline of time 7,8,11,59,60
Drucker, Peter 27,55

Eden, Anthony 122
Edison, Thomas 138
efficiency 46,65
80/20 rule 75,76
Einstein, A. 4, 138
Eisenhower, General 138
electronic mail 89
endorphins 140
energy 136,137,150
energy curve 70,71
escapism 56
estimating time required 59
exceptional tasks 125
exercise 139-140

failure, causes of 53
family 141
fatigue, physical and mental
                    69,70,71
    to remedy 70,71
Filofax system 58, Appendix B
Fisher, Admiral Lord 119
flexibility 54,60,64,71,74,102
Ford, Henry 9
France 7
Franklin, Benjamin 8,14,26,41

Gandhi, Mahatma 143
getting up early 71,135
goals 50,51,53,54,140,151 (see also
    objectives characteristics of 50

Goethe 130
good time management habits 13

Hale, Sir Matthew 7
Harrison's Chronometer 6
Hazlitt, William 4
health 135,150,151
heart disease 138,145
helicopter vision 47,54
high-quality time 67
Hitler's diaries 124
holidays 135,141-142,150
Hounsfield, Godfrey 130
Hugo, Victor 58

illusions of time 5
information collecting 75,89
insomnia 74,138
International Thomson Organisation
    124,125
interruptions 62,87-88,89,91,135
    damage-control hints 87-88,91
interviews 89-90, 93
Italians 7

James, William 40
Japanese managers 33
Jellicoe, Earl 119
Jerome, J K 14
Jewish religion 142
jogging 140
Johnson, Dr Samuel 41

Kennedy, President 36,37,138

Landes, David 5
leadership
    31,33,103,104,113,114,116,117,
                124,125,137,143
Lee, Ivy 61
life expectancy 11
living in the present 56-57
Livingstone, Sir Richard 143

long hours 135,141
lung cancer 138

Macbeth 137
MacDonald, George 76
manager's time 32-34
mantra 143
marginal time 127,134
Marks and Spencer 83
Marks, Sir Simon 83
measuring time 4,5,99
    artificial clocks — see clocks
    natural events 5
    nature's clock 5
meditation 142,143,144,145,149,150
meetings 20,21,22,26,32,33,
                58,59,86,93-109,151
    action to be taken 104,105,106
    agenda 99-100,101-102,103
    analysis of 99
    chairman 102-5,106,109
    cost of 97-8, 108
    making effective 107
    minutes
        101-102,104,105-106,109
    preparation for 99,100,101,109
    time-effective 22,99,108
    time limits 26,94,102
    timetabling 101-102
    types of 94-95,99,103,108
    visual aids 100
mental roadblocks 72
mental condition 135,136,142
middle-term planning 45-54,151
million pound idea 81
minutes 21,101-102,104,105-106,109
mismanager, case of the 18-20
mismanaging 18-20
moon, reaching the 37

moonlighting 74-75,76,138
morale 136
Moslem religion 142
motivation 53,126
motive power 24
Mussolini, B 123,137

Napoleon 34,137
nature's clock 5
nervous breakdowns 145,146
Nietzche, Friedrich 60
No - learning to say 62-63,65
Northwestern Mutual Life
    Insurance Company 86

objectives
        22-4,26,32,34,46,48,49,50,51,
        52,53,54,58,73,94,99,101,140,153
    checklist of good objectives 50
    characteristics of 50
    long-term 35-43
    setting objectives 53,54
offices
    automation 89
    design 79
    efficiency 19,20,26
    lighting 78,79
    organisation 78,151
    time effectiveness 77-91
    work area arrangement 78
operational planning
        36,45,46,47,48,49,51,55
over-commitment

paperwork 19,28,32,33,81-4
    Marks and Spencer method 83
    million pound idea 81,91
Pareto principle 75
Parkinson's Law 52,94,102
Pascal, B 145
Pasteur, L 75-76
pecking order 96

performance effective
        1,24,27,30,34,46,61,62,64,67,114
    high 68,69
philosophy of time 8,56
physcial fitness 135,136,141,142
Pilkington, Sir Alastair 129
planner chart 58
planning
        33,34,35,36-8,47,48,55,54,57,151
    life planning 36-8
    wide-angle planning 47,48
planning/implementation ratio 49
pocket watch 6,7
policies 41,42,94,121,153
    persoanl 57,70
policy-making 42,96
politeness 63
politics 145
poor delegator, case of the 15-18
prayer 142,143
pressures 2,28,65,143,147
Priestley, J B 141
prime time 68,69,70,71,72,75
priorities
        23,26,30,31,32,59,60,61,63,65,
        90,125,139,141,148,150,153
    paperwork 81-82
problems 13-26,32,43
    analysis 73,74,75
    recurring 32
procrastination 13-15,26,60,82,83
procrastinator, case of the 13-14
progress review 53,54
Protestants 7
psychology of time 4
Puritans 7,8,11
prupose 23,26,51,99
purpose, sense of 43

quality control of time 67,151

quality of time 67,135,142
quartz technology 6

radio 132
rate of change of time 4
rational management practice 123
reading effectively 84,85,91
reality 56-7
recreation 56,141
relationships 153,154
relativity theory 4
religion 7,142,143
reviewing performance 53-4,47
rhythm of life, natural 69,70,71
risk taking 123
round table 80,96
routines 41,42,51,52

St Augustine 4
St Mark's Cathedral, Venice 6
salary/time ratio (table) 97
Schwab, Charles M 61
secretary 19,58,89,91,105,132
self-discipline 29,141
self-fulfilment 41
self-improvement programme 24
    exercise 108
senior executives 32-3
sense of time 1,27-34,151
Shakespeare, W 39,137
Shell Oil Company 47,80
    managerial qualities (table) 47
silence, need for 143,145,150
sleep 136,137-8, 150
smoking 138-9
speed, effect on time 4
speed rading courses 85
staff training 22-4,120,121
standards 154
Steinberg, Dr Jonathan 64
strategic goals (also see objectives)
    36,37,39,41,43,45,46,49,53,54,55

stress 145,50
    causes of 147-8
    controlling 148-50
    disease 74-5
    symptoms 146,147,150
success criteria 52
success, limited 53
sundial 5,6
superpower relations 37
supply of time 10
Switzerland 6,7
systems 19,20
    paperwork 19

tactical planning 41,49,55,64
teachers 29
teamwork 77,114
telephone control 85-6,91
    batching calls 86
    call-back system 88
television 132-3
Temple, Archbishop William
                        137,142
Tennyson, Alfred Lord 130
Thatcher, Margaret 137-8
Theosophy 142
thinking, types of operational
                36,45,46,47,48,4,51,55
    strategic
        36,37,39,41,43,45,46,49,53,54,55
    tactical 41,49,55,64
Thomson of Fleet, Lord 122,123,124
Thoreau, Henry D 26,65
time
    /benefit ratio 59
    /change continuum 35/6,146
    fanatic 63-4
    management, concept of 3,151
    management skills 94,149,150

management tools
7,27,37,58,63,85
nature of 3
norms 51,52
planner chart 58
saving techniques 2,17
threat 21
trpas 21
use 30,31,34
wasting 2,19,34,77,97,144
"time is money" 8-10,11
Time Log 27,28,29,30,31,33,86
symbols to use 29
Toyota 33
training courses 22-4
Transcendental Meditation 142-3
Trollope, Anthony 131
Truman, President 113,138
trusting subordinates see delegation
Twain, Mark 149
tycoons 136

unclear objectives 24

understanding time 3,4
unexpected, time for 64

value judgements 56,60
value of time 5,8,9,11,28,125
values 39,40,41,43,64,112,148,153

Walker, Peter 145
watches (general) 8
Wellington, Duke of 14
White House 39
Winton, John 119
work addiction 141
work breaks 70-71
worry 149,150
wrist watch 6
writing effectively 84,85,91

Yoga 142

Zen-Buddhism 142